100 INSTANT DISCUSSION STARTERS

*This book is dedicated to
Adam and Jefferson*

100 Instant Discussion Starters

JOHN BUCKERIDGE

KINGSWAY PUBLICATIONS
EASTBOURNE

ISBN 0 85476 807 6

Published by
KINGSWAY PUBLICATIONS
Lottbridge Drove, Eastbourne, BN23 6NT, England.
E-mail: books@kingsway.co.uk

Designed and produced for the publishers by
Bookprint Creative Services, P.O. Box 827, BN21 3YJ, England.
Printed in Great Britain.

Contents

Acknowledgements

Several stories which appear in this book are adapted from a regular column 'It Must Be True' which appears in *The Week*. This weekly periodical is an excellent source of stories and summaries of the past week's news and is available from most large newsagents.

Some of these stories have appeared in an adapted form in *Youthwork* magazine in its regular 'Talking Point' column. For a complimentary copy of this magazine write to Youthwork, PO Box 17911, London SW1E 5ZR. To subscribe, phone: 01903 821082. Alternatively, check out the *Youthwork* magazine web site at: www.youthwork.co.uk

I first came across a small number of stories in this collection on the web. A few actually happened to me! As for the rest, they first appeared in newspapers, e-zines and magazines from across the world. Where possible I have quoted sources. However, sometimes I couldn't trace the origin. If I have failed to credit you as the source of any of these stories, I apologise. Please do let me know and I'll arrange for a credit to appear in any subsequent reprint. Names have been changed in some stories to avoid embarrassment.

John Buckeridge

Discussion Starter Do's and Don'ts!

Did Jesus have a hard time with the disciples? Were they distracted as easily as the adults and young people in your church? Halfway through the Sermon on the Mount did Philip ask Jesus, 'Do we have to write this down?' Did John add, 'My pen doesn't work'? Would Matthew have left halfway through the talk to go to the toilet? Did James interrupt with an irrelevant question? And would Bartholomew have complained, 'This has nothing to do with real life'? I don't know. But I do know that communicating to a mixed-age, multi-cultural audience, or to young people at the youth group, isn't easy. This book aims to help.

I chose 100 stories which I believe, when well told, will hold attention and provoke informed discussion. What's more, I've done a lot of the hard work for you by linking them into themes and listing Bible references they could apply to. So whether you're starting with a topic or working through a passage of Scripture, there should be loads of discussion triggers here to interest and stimulate.

But before you dive in, read the rest of this introduction to get some tips on discussion starter do's and don'ts.

Your job is to inspire and engage your listeners with a story, and secondly to act as a catalyst in discussion. These discussion starters may be 'instant' in that they're ready for use, but your own personal preparation is vital. Pray and ask for God's help. Then rehearse the story, reading it out loud several times. Although these stories stand up on their own, sometimes you may be linking them into a wider talk. If so, work hard on that link so it flows easily. Then read through the discussion triggers – you will want to adapt these and make them your own. You may want to add some questions of your own, or apply them more directly to the lives of your group.

Try reading the Bible passages in more than one version of the Bible, summarising the main points in your own words to get hold of what you think the scriptures are saying. Finally, get out a concordance and a commentary to see what light they can shed. The temptation is to bypass prayer and personal study and go straight to the so-called experts for help. This is a mistake, as it reduces the opportunity for the Holy Spirit to inspire and instruct you. Your delivery may also come across as stilted and second-hand if it lacks your original input.

Get them talking

The diagram opposite shows four types of group discussion.These stories are not collected together to help you give a lecture (1), or hold a conversation between you and the most spiritual member of the group which the others overhear (2). It shouldn't be a question-and-answer session with you in the role of inquisitor, and you are not there to impress people with your story-telling or with the extent of your Bible knowledge (3). Nor is it a no-holds-barred argument or shouting match. Ideally, the ensuing discussion (and Bible study) should involve every member equally (4).

You should act as a facilitator, occasionally directing or summing up the discussion (what it means and the implications for living today), and then stimulating further discussion on the story, the questions raised and the Bible passages.

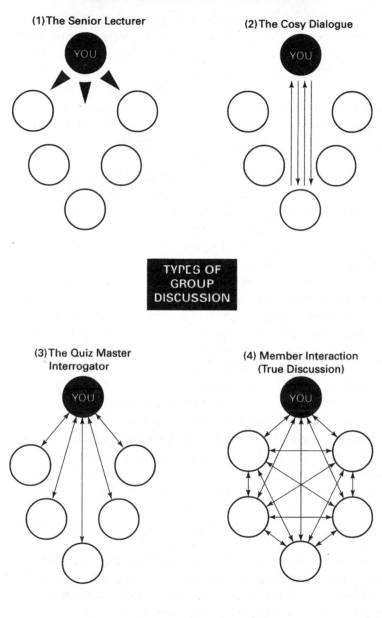

(1) The Senior Lecturer

(2) The Cosy Dialogue

TYPES OF
GROUP
DISCUSSION

(3) The Quiz Master
Interrogator

(4) Member Interaction
(True Discussion)

To be a good group facilitator you need to practise your listening skills. Many claim that the present generation knows less about the Bible than ever before. The clamour to teach Scripture has led some to adopt an aggressive 'teach them at all costs' style, which produces little or no dialogue between 'us and them'. Worse still, it produces little dialogue, interest and interaction between the young adult and the Bible. The underlying message in the Bible teaching style of many is, 'I'll teach – you listen.'

I believe we need to listen to and respect the opinion of the people we communicate with. Swiftly correcting what we see as heresy with a rebuke or a 'No, that's not the right answer' will only alienate our audience from our message. A more relaxed approach, where we listen to others, will help earn us the platform where we are listened to.

At times we will need to state clearly the Bible's position on fundamental truths. On certain black and white issues the Bible is plain and we must not muzzle God's word. However, that is no excuse for not listening to the words and the message behind the words of your group. A secure facilitator will feel able to stand back from a study when the discussion ignites, only seeking to comment when the discussion is running out of steam or is in need of summary, before pointing it in a new direction.

Focusing their attention on what the Bible actually says is worth a thousand of your words of wisdom! The use of carefully worded questions can help stimulate thought, study and discussion. Invariably the quality of your questions will depend on the level of your preparedness.

Questions, questions, questions

Questions are your basic tool to get the group to look at the passage, think about it and discover its meaning. Jesus frequently used this method. This book supplies an application with each story, which includes questions.

- DO try to anticipate the group's response to the questions.

- DON'T ask a question too abruptly.

- DO ask specific questions that are not too broad.

- DON'T ask abstract questions such as, 'How do your feelings compare with a butterfly struggling to emerge from its cocoon?'

- DO lead the group forward – questions should suggest an interesting road ahead, not a dead end.

- DON'T ask long and involved questions – if a question isn't brief and clear, break it up into a couple of statements.

- DO affirm a comment or answer.

- DON'T ask personal questions that might cause embarrassment.

- DO occasionally 'listen and reflect' following an answer, e.g. 'So what you're saying is . . .' This technique checks on your understanding of what was said and sums up the debate so far.

- DON'T allow the group to talk over the top of each other. Helping the group to actively listen to each other is a vital social skill to encourage.

When studying a Bible passage, prepare questions of observation, significance and application.

- Questions of observation get the group to search for the facts.

- Questions of significance make the group examine the meanings of words, phrases, actions and verses and the connection between them. Your questions should help them link the lessons of the passage with the biblical truths they already know.

- Questions of application challenge them to use mind and imagination to see the relevance of the truth they have learned. The group may not allow you to use these carefully prepared questions. Often they will jump to the heart of the matter before you ask. That doesn't matter – the point is, be prepared.

Discussion wheel

Use the diagram below to help you ask the right questions which will dig out the facts, meanings and implications.

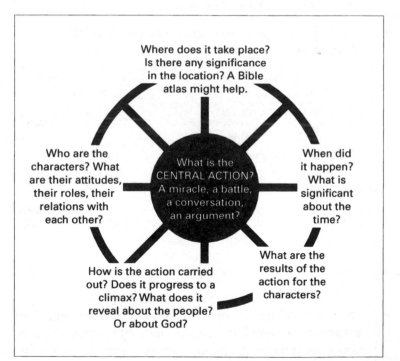

Where does it take place? Is there any significance in the location? A Bible atlas might help.

Who are the characters? What are their attitudes, their roles, their relations with each other?

What is the CENTRAL ACTION? A miracle, a battle, a conversation, an argument?

When did it happen? What is significant about the time?

How is the action carried out? Does it progress to a climax? What does it reveal about the people? Or about God?

What are the results of the action for the characters?

Creative approaches to group Bible study

Role play

If your group is comfortable with role play, use a Bible story (e.g. from the Gospels) and assign everyone in the group a part as one of the characters. If you have more people than characters, they can either double up, so that two people take on one character, or you can get the rest to play the part of the crowd.

Ask everyone to close their eyes while you read the story out loud. Ask them to concentrate on thinking how their character feels as the story unfolds. You may stop during the story or you may prefer to wait until the conclusion before asking each character in turn to describe their feelings of anger, surprise, thankfulness etc. Encourage interaction between characters in role.

Location Bible studies

Make the Bible study come alive by reading and studying stories in their original context, e.g. read Luke 8 (Jesus calms the storm) in a boat on a lake, or talk about God's power to create the stars (Psalm 8) on a midnight picnic. This requires considerable forward-planning and depends on site availability, but will certainly make the study memorable.

Buzz groups

Appoint research groups of two to four people who tackle one question each. Each group elects a scribe to report back after ten minutes.

Swedish method

This is applicable to parables, psalms and sections of epistles, and is useful in an emergency if the leader falls ill. Everyone receives a 10cm × 15cm card with five symbols on the left side. After reading through the Bible passage, each person writes on the card next to the appropriate symbol (top to bottom) the following:

- What the passage says about God.

- What the passage says about human nature.

- A new insight.

- Something which is unclear or a question which arises from the text.

- A command or action to obey.

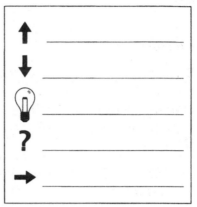

Share your findings in a general discussion.

Rewrite the Bible

Ask your group to put the Bible passage into their own words. If the passage includes a story, this can be rewritten in a twenty-first-century setting. This works especially well with a parable. Encourage them to use modern words and phrases, but stick to the original meaning or message of the passage. The story could even be turned into a poem, rap, pictures or symbols. Feed back and share interpretations. Agree on what was the most important message or concept from the passage.

Fill in the blanks

Choose a Bible passage from the epistles which teaches an important Christian doctrine, or choose a Bible study which your group is unlikely to know about. Write the story out on a worksheet, a flipchart pad or OHP, but leave some blanks. Let individuals decide what words they think are appropriate to fill in the blanks. Read out their answers, then read out the original Bible version. Compare the differences and talk about why Jesus or the biblical author chose the words they did.

Creature comforts

Selecting an appropriate location for a discussion is crucial. Get it wrong and no matter how riveting the material, people will be distracted. Here are my top tips on getting the environment right for a group discussion or Bible study.

1. Choose a room which comfortably fits the numbers expected. A huge draughty hall with only five people in it will feel cold and intimidating. With twenty-five crammed into a tiny front room the discomfort factor will overrule everything else.

2. Arrange the room and seating so that everyone can establish eye contact with the rest of the group and can easily be heard.

3. Get the temperature right. Shivering in overcoats or sweating like pigs is not very conducive to creating a relaxed learning atmosphere.

4. Reduce distraction by ensuring that a chattering toddler or a ringing telephone will not interrupt at a vital moment.

5. Leave a chair for the latecomer. If a newcomer arrives late and discovers the only space available is on the middle of a settee between two members of the opposite sex, he or she is unlikely to come again. Teenagers are especially aware of the need for personal space. Invade that zone and they feel embarrassed and awkward.

6. If comfort must be compromised, make sure you're the one who has the uncomfortable chair; or if the sun is shining through a window, you're the one squinting because the sun is in your face.

7. Don't overrun the agreed finishing time. Fatigue or the need to be somewhere else makes a long meeting bad news.

The Discussion Starters

1 A Modern-Day Fairy Tale

Once upon a time, in a land far away, a beautiful, independent, self-assured princess encountered a frog as she sat contemplating ecological issues by the shores of an unpolluted pond in a verdant meadow near her castle.

The frog hopped into the princess' lap and with a croaky voice said: 'Elegant Lady, I was once a handsome prince until an evil witch cast a spell on me. One kiss from you, however, and I will turn back into the dapper, young prince that I once was. Then, my darling, we can marry and live together with my mother in my castle beyond the valley, where you can prepare my meals, clean my clothes, bear my children, and for ever feel grateful and happy doing so.'

That night, as the princess dined sumptuously on a meal of lightly sautéed frog's legs, seasoned in a white wine and shallot cream sauce, she laughed to herself and thought, 'I don't think so!'

APPLICATION

Not quite the usual 'happy ever after' ending, was it? But the expectations, aspirations and hopes that women have in Western society today are very different compared to fifty years ago. Equal rights, equal pay and equal opportunities mean that women are not financially dependent on men.

However, many working women feel that their husband/partner expects them to do the housework, cooking and other chores – even though they also work full time. Although there are a growing number of 'new men' who do their share around the house, many couples still fulfil certain 'traditional' roles, and in most homes women cook while men do the DIY.

Are men and women equal or different – or can they be both? If you have children, would you be happy to buy your son a My Little Pony toy or your daughter an Action Man to play with?

The Bible teaches that people – no matter what their race, colour, background or gender – are all equal in God's sight. The competitive and aggressive 'battle of the sexes' is a result of our fallen sinful nature. Men and women should love and honour each other. Co-operation and mutual respect should be the hallmark of our relationships with the opposite sex; we shouldn't hide behind false stereotypes but instead strive towards biblical standards of manliness and womanliness.

THEMES

Equality
Gender
Marriage
Sexism

BIBLE REFERENCES

Genesis 1:27; 2:21–23; 5:2
Matthew 19:4
Mark 10:6
1 Corinthians 11:9
Galatians 3:28

2 Asking God For . . .

Little Sammy was lying on the sweet, green grass of a wide meadow on a warm, spring day. Puffy, white clouds rolled overhead and as Sammy looked at them he pondered on their shape. Soon, he began to think about God.

'God, are you really there?' Sammy said out loud.

To his astonishment a voice came from the clouds. 'Yes, Sammy. What can I do for you?'

Seizing the opportunity, Sammy asked, 'God? What is a million years like to you?'

Knowing that little Sammy couldn't begin to understand the concept of infinity, God replied, 'A million years to me, Sammy, is like a minute.'

'Oh,' said Sammy. 'Well, then, what's a million pounds like to you?'

'A million pounds to me, Sammy, is like a penny.'

'Wow!' remarked Sammy, getting an idea. 'You're so generous, can I have one of your pennies?'

God replied, 'Of course, Sammy! Just a minute.'

APPLICATION

Sometimes we don't get the answer to our prayers that we want or expect. It may be because we are asking out of very selfish motives, or because we are asking God for things which will harm us or be bad for our spiritual development.

'The purpose of prayer is to find God's will and to make that will our prayer' (Catherine Marshall).

'Gain all you can, save all you can, give all you can'
(Margaret Thatcher quoting John Wesley).
   If you could ask God three questions, what would they be?

THEMES

Character of God
Infinity
Money
Prayer
Time

BIBLE REFERENCES

Psalm 90:4; 119:14, 72
Ecclesiastes 5:10
Jeremiah 29:12
Matthew 6:21; 21:22
Luke 16:14
John 14:13–14
1 Timothy 3:3; 6:10
2 Timothy 3:2
Hebrews 13:5
James 4:3; 5:16–18
2 Peter 3:8
1 John 3:22; 5:14–15

3 Asleep at Your Desk 6·30 3/07.

What do you do if you get caught sleeping at your desk at work or at college? Do you tell the truth or spout some lame reason? Here are a few excuses some people have offered:

'They told me at the blood bank this might happen.'

'Whew! I must've left the top off the Tippex bottle. You probably got here just in time. Thanks for stopping me slipping into a coma!'

If your boss at work catches you snoozing, you could try: 'I wasn't sleeping! I was meditating on the mission statement and envisioning a new paradigm.' Or even: 'I was testing my keyboard for drool resistance.'

Given that the best form of defence is attack, if you're feeling daring you could say: 'Why did you interrupt me? I had almost figured out a solution to our biggest problem.'

A more feelings-oriented approach might be the lame excuse: 'The coffee machine is broken . . .'

All of these excuses are lies, of course, but for the Christian snoozing at his desk, the biggest whopper would be: '. . . in Jesus' name. Amen.'

APPLICATION

Honesty is the best policy. Is this true? What's the lamest excuse you've ever heard?

THEMES
Excuses
Honesty
Sleep

BIBLE REFERENCES

Exodus 18:21
Leviticus 19:35–36
Deuteronomy 25:13–16
2 Samuel 7:28
1 Kings 9:4–5
Psalms 15:1–2; 19:7; 33:4
Proverbs 11:1; 17:26; 29:10, 27
Isaiah 59:14–15
Jeremiah 26:15
Ezekiel 45:10
Zechariah 8:16–17
John 4:23–24; 18:23
Romans 1:18
1 Corinthians 5:8
2 Corinthians 4:2
Ephesians 4:15, 25
Philippians 4:8
1 Peter 2:22

4 Bigger and Better

A sightseeing bus was travelling around London and the driver was pointing out places of interest. As they passed St Paul's Cathedral, he mentioned that it took years to build and was considered Sir Christopher Wren's masterpiece. While everyone was admiring the cathedral, a little old woman on the back seat of the coach spoke up: 'In Doncaster we could have built the same building and finished it in six months!'

The next sight on the tour was the Millennium Dome in Greenwich. The bus driver explained that it had cost many millions to build and had taken two years to complete. The woman said: 'In Doncaster we would have done it for less money, and it would have been finished much sooner.'

The tour finally came to Trafalgar Square, and the driver passed slowly by without saying a word. The old woman was curious. 'Hey!' she shouted to the driver. 'What's that tall column surrounded by massive fountains and stone lions back there?' The driver looked out of the window, waited a minute and then said, 'I have no idea, madam. It wasn't there yesterday.'

APPLICATION

Some people make claims or promises which are based on an exaggerated affirmation of their ability to fulfil the promise. Peter told Jesus, 'I am ready to go with you to prison and to death' (Luke 22:33), but within twenty-four hours he had failed dismally to keep his exaggerated and boastful claim of faithfulness.

Why do people boast or exaggerate about their home town, their own abilities or their upbringing? (Fear, envy, pride, self-pity, etc.)

Certain professions are notorious for employing people who exaggerate. Name some. (Second-hand car salesmen, salesmen/women in general, estate agents, marketing/PR, market traders, American evangelists!)

THEMES

Boasting
Exaggeration

BIBLE REFERENCES

Psalm 10:2–6; 12:3–4; 94:4
Romans 1:29–30
1 Corinthians 3:18–23
2 Timothy 3:1–2
James 4:13–16
1 John 2:16

24/11/02 WIC

5   Blame It on the Genes

Whether or not you are likely to become a compulsive gambler may all be down to the genes you inherit from your parents, according to recent research. Scientists who studied over 3,000 twins say evidence is growing that addiction to gambling on horse racing and the roulette wheel – once thought to be purely a social condition – is inherited. They claim that one day researchers may be able to identify a 'gambling gene' which would open the door to new forms of treatment for gamblers.

Research into twins has discovered that the chance of becoming a serious gambler is much higher if your twin is also addicted to betting. The link is even stronger if the twins are identical, as they share the same set of genes from their parents.

About 3 in every 100 people are seriously addicted to gambling in Britain, and with the options in legalised gambling having increased in recent years, the problem is likely to get worse.

Other studies have suggested there may be genes which make people more likely to become hardened smokers. Most controversial, though, is the evidence some researchers claim to have discovered which shows a 'gay gene' that predisposes people to being homosexually inclined.

APPLICATION

Are humans controlled by genes, hormones, feelings and instincts in the same way as animals and birds, or do we have

31

the ability to make choices and decisions for ourselves? Are we hostage to our genes, or are we in control?

How would you feel if a member of your family was raped and murdered, and when the person responsible for this evil deed was caught by police his defence to the court was 'It's not my fault, my instincts and my genes made me do it'? Isn't it a rather convenient excuse for the rapist, murderer, drug addict or liar to say 'I was made this way'?

We are who we are as a result of a combination of factors: inherited genes, gifts and traits; the impact of our environment, friends, teachers and society at large; plus the unique inner person – the essence of 'you' that is made in the image of God. Although we can be conditioned and influenced by these other factors, we are still our own person, and as such the Bible teaches that we are responsible to God and our fellow men/women for our actions. One day we will be judged by God and separated 'sheep from goats', 'believers from unbelievers'.

THEMES

Addiction
Choice
Gambling
Genes
Homosexuality
Personal responsibility

BIBLE REFERENCES

Deuteronomy 24:16; 30:19
Joshua 24:15
1 Kings 18:21
Job 19:4
Jeremiah 31:30

Ezekiel 18:20
Luke 12:48
Romans 14:12
1 Corinthians 7:24
1 Peter 4:4–5

6   Boffins' Forecast

One boffin has predicted that by the year 2020 Baroness Thatcher will have died, been frozen, then brought back to life to lead the country! Another forecasts that the M25 will have thirty-five lanes and will be used by fast, efficient cars. Unfortunately these will be completely silent, and pedestrian casualties will soar by 1,000 per cent in towns and cities.

These predictions were made in a competition organised by *New Scientist* magazine in 1993. One of the weirdest winning ideas suggested gene thieves would steal part of Elvis Presley's body to clone the star from his DNA.

More recently, popular science magazines have been crammed with predictions of scenarios for the first twenty years of the next millennium. These have included: the discovery of an enzyme which will halt the ageing process; making contact with aliens; nuclear conflict between Pakistan and India; increased computerisation and automation putting millions more on the dole; and global warming causing major climactic changes.

APPLICATION

What new developments do you predict will happen by the year 2020?

The Bible contains several predictions about the future, the return of Jesus and the end of the world. Jesus is returning for his church, for the judgement of the whole world and to prevent the total destruction of the world. The Bible teaches that this 'Second Coming' is something all

Christians should look forward to and expect. We cannot predict the time when these things will happen, but the Bible does teach that it will be sudden and 'like a thief in the night' (1 Thessalonians 5:2).

In the next-to-last verse of the Bible (Revelation 22:20) John, who has seen a vision of the end of the world, prays, 'Come, Lord Jesus.' Are you as keen as John was to see Jesus return?

THEMES

End of the world
Future
Prophecy

BIBLE REFERENCES

Matthew 24:3–51; 26:64
Mark 13
Luke 12:40
1 Corinthians 4:5
1 Thessalonians 4:13–5:11
2 Timothy 4:1
Titus 2:13
James 5:8
Revelation 3:11; 16:15; 22:20

7 Burning Blunder

An American woman misheard her husband's instructions on how to turn up the central heating and ended up burning down their house. Edith Bloom, 77, of Minnesota, had cold feet and hands and couldn't manage to make the boiler work, so she phoned her son at work for advice. He told her to 'set the thermostat higher' but she thought he said 'set the thermostat on fire', which she duly achieved, using a blow-torch. Although she managed to escape the ensuing fire, the house was completely destroyed.

APPLICATION

We all make mistakes. Sadly, Mrs Bloom's poor hearing caused her to make a mistake which resulted in the loss of her home. Some mistakes have minor consequences, some can make all the difference in the world. The Bible warns against being led astray by false prophets, following myths and old wives' tales, and falling away from the true faith – these mistakes can have eternal consequences.

God always hears us. He hears us when we pray to him, and when we grumble, and he hears the cry of the oppressed.

When we hear the word of God we must respond. However, it is important to discern correctly. Young Samuel heard a voice but didn't know it was God. In time, as God spoke to him again and again, he became known as a true prophet who heard and discerned wisely the ways and words of the Lord.

God's words need to be heard and then accurately acted upon.

THEMES

Error
Hearing
Mistakes

BIBLE REFERENCES

Exodus 3:7; 16:7–9, 11–12
Numbers 11:1; 12:1–2; 14:27
2 Samuel 22:7
Psalms 3:4; 94:9
Isaiah 65:24
Jeremiah 23:13; 50:6
Matthew 7:24–27; 13:16–23; 22:29; 24:4, 11, 24
Luke 21:8
John 5:24; 11:41–42
Acts 20:30
Ephesians 1:13
1 Timothy 4:7
2 Timothy 4:4
Titus 1:14
Hebrews 4:2
James 1:22–24; 3:2; 5:4
1 Peter 3:12
2 Peter 3:17

8 Burning Passion

During worldwide Kurdish demonstrations, the name of one 15-year-old, Nejla Kanteper, was on the front page of every newspaper and headed most TV news bulletins, along with the shocking picture of her burning body. Nejla set herself on fire to bring attention to the plight of the Kurdish people following the arrest by Turkish authorities of the PKK leader Abdullah Ocalan.

The teenager suffered 30 per cent burns to her back, neck and arms. Her family, like many other Kurds, fled from Turkey to Britain to seek asylum. She has several uncles who were tortured in Turkish prisons for their support of the PKK, a faction which has an armed campaign to establish a separate Kurdistan.

Despite the pain from her burns and the need for surgery, Nejla's mother said the teenager had no regrets about what she had done. Mrs Kanteper said her daughter had told her not to cry, and said she did not want sympathy.

APPLICATION

When your family has lost everything, including some relatives, and when you have suffered a terrifying journey out of a country where you were being persecuted, and where your people still suffer injustice, you will feel an intense passion. Some people have strong ideals and believe change is possible – not everyone is cynical.

Is there anything for which you would be prepared to suffer and maybe even die? The word 'martyr' comes from

the Greek word 'witness', which illustrates how dying for the
gospel is the supreme form of witness for the Christian faith.

THEMES

Idealism
Martyrdom

BIBLE REFERENCES

1 Kings 19:10
Matthew 10:39; 14:10–12; 23:30–34
Mark 6:27–29
Luke 9:9; 11:47–49; 21:16
John 16:2; 21:18–19
Acts 7:52–60; 12:2; 22:20
Romans 8:35–36; 11:3
1 Corinthians 13:3
Hebrews 11:35, 37
James 5:6
Revelation 2:10, 13; 6:9–10; 11:7; 13:15; 16:6; 17:6; 20:4

9   Caught Out   2/3/1??.

Wanda Ellis thought her armed robbery of a petrol station in Louisiana had been successful. She had achieved her aim of gaining a lot of cash and had escaped capture.

However, the next day as she relaxed in front of the television, she was horrified to see pictures of the station being robbed on the local news report. Thinking that it was only a matter of time before the police identified her, she walked into the nearest police station and gave herself up. Only after she had made a written and verbal confession did the detective reveal that the film footage she had seen on TV was a reconstruction featuring a police officer and not her!

APPLICATION

Imagine the horrible feeling Wanda must have experienced when she watched the TV news and thought she had seen herself. Now imagine how much worse she felt when she realised that she had given herself away! Have you ever been in a similar situation – thinking you've got away with something and only later discovering that you've been found out?

If criminals knew that their every move was being recorded on video and available to the police and courts, would they become reformed characters? Is this the answer to rising levels of criminality – to put CCTV cameras everywhere?

Even though the use of CCTV cameras is growing, there are still many places where we like to feel we are alone and that our actions, words and thoughts will not be recorded.

The Bible teaches that God sees everything – even our thoughts. Does that make you feel reassured or afraid?

THEMES

Crime
Foolishness
Sin

BIBLE REFERENCES

Numbers 32:23
Psalms 51:4; 90:8; 119:11
Ecclesiastes 7:20
Daniel 4:27
Romans 3:23; 6:1
1 Corinthians 15:34
1 Timothy 5:24
James 4:17
1 John 2:1; 3:6

10 Changing Faces

Face transplants could technically be possible within five years, according to a leading American plastic surgeon.

Following the first ever hand transplant, which took place at a French hospital in October 1998, plastic surgeons are becoming more ambitious. According to Dr John Barker of the University of Louisville, Kentucky, the donors of a face transplant would be brain-dead people on life support machines, of the same age as the recipient. Surgeons would transplant the facial skin, muscles, nerves, and even lips.

In situations where a person's bones had been destroyed, such as mouth cancer or attempted suicides, the donor's bones could also be used to create a new base for the transplanted skin.

Dr Barker told *New Scientist* magazine that he believes face transplants will begin to take place by around 2003. The magazine warns: 'The idea of a new market emerging among the ageing rich for young faces is too awful to contemplate.' It adds: 'Besides, cosmetic surgeons can already transform the faces of the living. Ask Michael Jackson.'

APPLICATION

Would you be prepared to donate your face when you die? Do you feel this is any different from donating internal organs such as heart, kidneys or even eyes?

What makes a person a unique individual? How much of that 'identity' is to do with their face?

The Bible says that in the end every human being will see God face to face (Revelation 22:4). How do you feel about that?

THEMES

Appearance
Identity
Recognition
Transplants

BIBLE REFERENCES

Genesis 32:30
Exodus 33:20–23
1 Corinthians 13:12
Revelation 22:4

11   Chop Chop

Before he was wheeled to the operating theatre, William King joked with nursing staff at a hospital in Tampa, Florida, urging them to be sure they knew which of his feet they were going to amputate.

Sadly, the surgeon made a catastrophic mistake. When the 51-year-old awoke from the anaesthetic he found, to his horror, that he still had his gangrenous right foot, but was missing his healthy left one!

Eventually he had to have both legs removed just below the knee. The surgeon agreed to pay $250,000 compensation.

Now the hospital has introduced a new policy of writing with thick pen the word 'No' on patients' limbs which are not to be amputated!

APPLICATION

What's the biggest mistake you have made in your life? We all make mistakes and we have to live with the consequences of them.

Would you have been able to forgive the surgeon? Is there anyone who has wronged you, that you still need to forgive?

THEMES

Forgiveness
Mistakes

BIBLE REFERENCES

1 Chronicles 21:8
Proverbs 21:5
Haggai 1:5
Matthew 5:23–24; 18:23–35
Mark 11:25
Romans 12:17–19
Ephesians 5:15

12   Crazy Preacher

When John Harding wanted to communicate the gospel to young people, he decided to use modern technology to aid his preaching. So he bought an £8,000 paramotor – a kind of powered parachute – to fly over a housing estate in Wiltshire, England.

'I wanted to preach at people with a megaphone,' he said. 'I wanted to try to get through to the kids on council estates and I needed something with street cred. I thought maybe that if they heard this voice booming out of the sky, they would think it was God.'

As if the idea of a birdman evangelist wasn't crazy enough, Mr Harding became a national source of scorn when a practice flight nearly ended in disaster. Instead of soaring over the estate in Salisbury, he lost height and had to weave between houses, lifting his legs up to clear garden fences. One resident, Mrs Margaret Blue, told newspaper reporters that the preacher flew so low she had serious fears he would collide with her bird table.

Although Mr Harding managed to land safely in a field, he was taken to court by the Civil Aviation Authority and fined £1,000 with £250 costs after admitting flying too close to a populated area.

Despite nearly disembowelling himself on garden furniture Mr Harding was dismissive of the incident, describing it as 'just a step on the way to the ministry'.

APPLICATION

Evangelism – or virtually anything else done in the name of the church – when done badly, or in a culturally insensitive way, is unhelpful and often makes subsequent attempts to communicate the good news more difficult. We must be careful that in our enthusiasm and eagerness to share the gospel, our strategy, words and actions do not make things worse rather than better!

'It seems to me easier to give sermons than to sit through them' (Rabbi Lionel Blue).

THEMES

Evangelism
Preaching

BIBLE REFERENCES

Isaiah 61:1
Matthew 4:23; 9:35; 10:7; 24:14
Mark 3:14; 6:12; 13:10; 16:15
Luke 9:2, 60; 24:47
Acts 5:42; 10:42; 14:7
Romans 15:20
1 Corinthians 1:17, 21; 9:16
Ephesians 3:8
2 Timothy 4:17

13   Cut the *%#^!!

Fed up with the bad language of the pupils in her school, a head teacher decided to ban swearing, with Saturday morning detention as a punishment for those found guilty of effing and blinding.

Rosemary Lewis, Head of Morton Upper School, said her ban reflected her dismay at the amount of foul language in everyday speech, with children being influenced by television, films and pop music.

'Youngsters are exposed to foul language at almost every turn and are starting to use the words almost without thinking,' she said.

Now any pupil caught swearing has to attend school in uniform for an hour on a Saturday morning to do class work under the supervision of a teacher. Anyone who doesn't turn up is punished by exclusion from normal classes with the stigma of being taught in a separate room on their own for a day.

The head claims 99 per cent of pupils support the policy and feel the school is a better place as a result.

APPLICATION

Would you welcome this rule in your local school?

'My mates swear to look cool.' Comment on this quote from a 12-year-old. For what other reasons do people swear or use offensive language?

If someone accidentally dropped something heavy on your foot, causing you sudden and sharp pain, would you be likely to swear?

Do you wish you could reduce or stop your swearing? What strategies would help?

THEMES

Profanity
Swearing

BIBLE REFERENCES

Exodus 20:7; 21:17
Deuteronomy 5:11
Proverbs 20:20; 25:28; 30:11
Matthew 5:34
Luke 6:28
Romans 12:14
James 3:10; 5:12

14 Double Dutch

Here are some signs and notices written in English and seen throughout the world. Where words are misspelled, these appear as on the original sign.

In a Bucharest hotel lobby: The lift is being fixed for the next day. During that time we regret that you will be unbearable.

On the menu of a Swiss restaurant: Our wines leave you nothing to hope for.

In a Rhodes tailor's shop: Order your summers suit. Because is big rush we will execute customers in strict rotation.

In an advertisement by a Hong Kong dentist: Teeth extracted by the latest Methodists.

In a Copenhagen airline ticket office: We take your bags and send them in all directions.

On the door of a Moscow hotel room: If this is your first visit to Russia, you are welcome to it.

In a Budapest zoo: Please do not feed the animals. If you have any suitable food, give it to the guard on duty.

In a Mexican hotel: The manager has personally passed all the water served here.

APPLICATION

The Bible teaches that the diversity of language came as a result of sin. However, the coming of the Spirit at Pentecost broke down the barriers of nationality and language.

Have you ever faced difficulties in making yourself understood to someone whose language you cannot understand?

THEMES

Language
Mistakes
Travel

BIBLE REFERENCES

Genesis 10:5; 11:1–9
Deuteronomy 28:49–50
Nehemiah 13:23–24
Psalms 55:9; 81:5
Isaiah 19:18; 28:11
Jeremiah 5:15
Ezekiel 3:5–6
Daniel 1:4
Mark 16:17
Acts 2:1–11; 10:44–48
1 Corinthians 12:10, 28; 14:10–11, 21

15   Dreamy DJ

Getting up early to present his daily radio breakfast show hadn't been a problem before – until one fateful day. Phil Barnes, the breakfast DJ on Sunderland-based SunFM, fell asleep for a full thirty minutes just after 7am. As Mr Barnes, who was in the studio on his own, dozed, the emergency music standby system took over to fill the silence!

Barnes was sleeping soundly until his furious boss arrived to wake him at 7.30am. After the show ended at 10am, he was fired.

The 26-year-old told reporters: 'One minute I was sitting there reading my advert list, the next I had my boss in the studio shouting at me to wake up. There was no one more angry with me than myself.'

APPLICATION

Ecclesiastes reminds us that there is a time for everything (3:1). We all need to sleep. However, there are also times when we need to be alert and fully awake. If we fail to sleep when we should and get tired, and then sleep when we should be alert, we will face disaster – just like the sleepy DJ. The discipline of getting regular sleep is important.

There is a direct spiritual parallel with the physical need to rest and sleep. Our spirits need refreshment and rest so that we are on guard against our spiritual enemy. If we fail to refresh our spirits by praying, reading the Bible and spending time worshipping God and being with God's people, our guard will be down and we will be more likely to doze in the face of danger. Giving in to temptation is just one of the likely outcomes of spiritual tiredness.

Jesus warned his followers to be alert because no one knows when he will return (Mark 13). Don't miss the signs of his coming. In 1 Thessalonians 5 it says that Christ's return will be sudden, 'like a thief in the night'. Don't be caught out like the sleeping DJ when the Master returns!

THEMES

Discipline
End of the world
Future
Second Coming
Sleep
Temptation

BIBLE REFERENCES

Judges 7:19–22
Psalm 3:5
Proverbs 6:10–11
Isaiah 21:6–8
Matthew 26:36–46
Mark 13:32–37
1 Thessalonians 5:1–11
1 Peter 5:8

16   Dying to be Arnie

For fourteen years Andreas Muenzer used drugs and pumped iron in his quest to have bigger muscles than Arnold Schwarzenegger. He eventually achieved his goal, but his obsession also killed him.

Each day he worked out at his local gym, sweating to lift weights to transform his torso into 232lb of bulging, rippling – and, to many, grotesque – muscle. Even after being named Germany's top bodybuilder, Muenzer kept a photograph of Schwarzenegger pinned to his bedroom wall to inspire him to keep on training.

Convinced that exercise alone would not allow him to fulfil his dream, he supplemented his diet with a daily cocktail of drugs to enhance muscle growth, including anabolic steroids, vitamins and mineral pills.

In March 1996, the bodybuilder reached the final of the Schwarzenegger Classics contest in the United States. But after he flew home his stomach, heart, kidneys and liver were found to be fatally damaged, and doctors blamed his death weeks later on the drugs he had taken. Source: *Daily Mail*

APPLICATION

What is the difference between ambition and obsession?

Dreams and ambitions are not bad things in themselves. However, when they become an obsession which people follow to the exclusion of all else, they can take over their entire existence and even put their lives in danger. Andreas

Muenzer's lifetime quest to become like his hero resulted in his own death.

If you had been a friend of Andreas, what would you have said or done to try to help him break free from his obsession? Are you, or is someone you know, in danger of becoming obsessive about something, or do you need to become less laid back and have more drive?

THEMES

Ambition
Dreams
Drugs
Obsession

BIBLE REFERENCES

Genesis 11:4
2 Samuel 15:1–4
Proverbs 6:16, 18
Mark 10:36–37
Galatians 5:19–21

17 Excuses, Excuses

As an excuse for arriving late at work, hitting an escaped buffalo during the car journey to the office must rank among the most weird. It may be strange, but it was true. That outlandish story is just one among a host of other unusual and more common excuses for being late for work or school.

A survey of people's early morning habits revealed that other excuses included: being abducted by aliens, the cat sleeping in, cows on the railway line, and breaking a tooth on a hard piece of toast.

Old favourites like a faulty alarm clock and problems with transport or the weather were the most common excuses.

APPLICATION

For some people, the thought of work brings pleasure, anticipation and fulfilment. For others it is a bore, a chore or something to put off. Jerome K. Jerome could probably relate to the latter when he wrote: 'I like work, it fascinates me. I can sit and look at it for hours.'

'Without work, all life goes rotten. But when work is soulless, life stifles and dies' (French existentialist writer Albert Camus).

Look at the Parable of the Great Banquet (Luke 14) and discuss people's excuses for non-attendance.

THEMES

Excuses
Lateness
Lies
Time
Work

BIBLE REFERENCES

2 Chronicles 31:21
Nehemiah 6:16
Psalm 104:23
Luke 14:15–24
Romans 1:20

18 Feel-Good Factors

Popeye's favourite food can increase your intelligence in old age according to medical experiments scientists have made on rats. Antioxidants in this leafy vegetable help repair damage to the brain caused by free radicals.

Giving blood is another health benefit. Scientists in Finland claim that donating a pint of blood helps you just as much as the recipient, since it reduces your levels of iron, which in excess can lead to heart attacks.

Regular attendance at church can also help your feel-good factor. American scientists have discovered that those who worship weekly are 40 per cent less likely to have dangerously high blood pressure.

Finally, there is good news for grubby kids. Having fewer baths and showers reduces a child's chance of getting asthma. A study of 14,000 children in England suggested that going without a bath helps children to develop a natural resistance to allergens before asthma sets in.

APPLICATION

We are whole beings. We need to take care of our physical, mental, emotional, social and spiritual selves in order to live healthy, balanced lives. Since our bodies are the temple of the Holy Spirit we should take care of ourselves – not to the point of over-indulgence, but we should not feel guilty about relaxing, spending time with God or our family and friends, reading, eating, or sleeping.

THEMES

Balance
Health – physical
Health – spiritual

BIBLE REFERENCES

Exodus 34:21
Leviticus 26:16
Deuteronomy 4:28; 28:21–22
Psalm 38:3–8
Proverbs 4:22
Jeremiah 8:15; 33:6
John 5:6–9
Acts 3:16
1 Corinthians 9:24–27
Ephesians 5:29
1 Thessalonians 5:23
1 Timothy 4:7–8
3 John 2

19   Feeling Good

What makes you feel good? Economic factors like having
plenty of money or a good job are no longer enough to
measure a person's quality of life, according to Tony Blair's
government. In 1998 the government revealed thirteen ways
to figure out the true feel-good factor. These included: economic growth, sustainable development, employment,
access to good health and education services, living in a nice
home, living in a clean environment, water quality, low air
pollution and reduced road congestion. Other factors were
slightly more surprising. One suggested that seeing wild
birds in your garden or near your home helped make people
happy.

APPLICATION

The Bible portrays both God and people as having emotions. Our feelings can be positive or negative and are
subject to change. True happiness and fulfilment are not
necessarily based on having positive feelings, according to
the Bible.

Happiness can be found in:

- Experiencing God's forgiveness (Psalm 32:1–2; Romans
  4:7–8)

- God's presence (Psalm 16:11; 1 Thessalonians 3:9)

- Human relationships (Genesis 30:13; 34:19; Song of
  Songs 4:10)

- Obeying God (Psalm 89:12; John 20:29)

- Suffering (Matthew 5:11–12; 1 Peter 3:14)

- Trusting God (Psalm 84:12; Galatians 3:9)

THEMES

Contentment
Feelings
Happiness

BIBLE REFERENCES

Genesis 30:13; 34:19
Psalms 16:11; 32:1–2; 84:12; 89:12
Song of Songs 4:10
Matthew 5:11–12
John 20:29
Romans 4:7–8
Galatians 3:9
1 Thessalonians 3:9
1 Peter 3:14

20 Fibber Caught Out

Two men applied for a job in a computer software company. The two applicants, having the same qualifications, were asked to take a test by the personnel manager. Upon completion of the test both men had failed to answer just one of the questions. The manager went to the second of the two and said, 'Thank you for your interest, but we've decided to give the job to the other final applicant.'

The rejected applicant said, 'Why are you rejecting me? We both got nine answers correct. What made you decide to take the other applicant when we both had the same qualifications and the same scores on the test?'

'We have made our decision not on the correct answers, but on the question neither of you could answer,' the personnel manager replied.

'And just how could one wrong answer be better than the other?' asked the rejected applicant.

'Simple,' the personnel manager replied. 'The other applicant wrote "I don't know" on question five. You wrote down, "Neither do I".'

APPLICATION

The personnel manager didn't need a huge amount of wisdom or discernment to discover who really deserved to get the job. The Bible describes Solomon as the wisest man ever to have lived. One of the examples it gives of his discernment is when he determined which of two women claiming to be the mother of a baby was the true mother (1 Kings 3:16–28).

Discernment is an important gift required for wise government, spiritual understanding and sound judgement to distinguish between good and evil, right and wrong. James 1:5 tells us: 'If any of you lacks wisdom, he should ask God, who gives generously to all without finding fault, and it will be given to him.'

Why do people lie and cheat? There is an old saying: 'Cheaters never prosper.' Do you agree?

THEMES

Cheating
Discernment
Lies
Wisdom

BIBLE REFERENCES

2 Samuel 14:17
1 Kings 3:16–28
Proverbs 15:21
Daniel 2:21
1 Corinthians 12:10; 14:29
James 1:5

6/1/02 P.

21 First Impressions

When Felix Hoffman created acetylsalicylic acid (aspirin) in 1897, his bosses at Bayer rejected it as useless and dangerous. The German chemical company was far more excited by another of Hoffman's discoveries that year, diacetylmorphine. Factory workers who had sampled it said the drug made them feel 'heroic', prompting the company to call its new wonder-drug 'heroin', and promote it as a cough remedy and a 'non-addictive alternative' to morphine.

Eventually Bayer conceded that aspirin had its uses and promoted the pair as the ultimate drug cocktail: aspirin for your headache, heroin for your cough!

Bayer stopped advertising heroin when they realised why people were coming back for more. The modest aspirin, however, continued to sell well – and medical uses beyond merely curing a headache were discovered. Today the world swallows 100 billion aspirin tablets a year and it has been dubbed the drug of the twentieth century.

Aspirin is used to prevent heart attacks, strokes, bowel cancers, leg thromboses, dementia, pre-eclamptic toxaemia in pregnant mothers, cataracts and blindness in diabetics. It is popular as an anti-inflammatory treatment for sufferers of rheumatoid arthritis and is as effective as opiates for relieving many types of severe pain. It is also pretty good for a hangover.

Not bad for a drug which was initially considered useless or, at best, a very poor second to a drug the 'experts' thought would make an effective cough medicine! Source: *Cover* magazine

APPLICATION

First impressions are important, but we can make mistakes. People or things can be dismissed as 'no good' when in fact they are 'very good' – like the record executive who heard a demo tape of the Beatles in the early 1960s and dismissed the band as no-hopers!

If you have ever been dismissed as useless or not up to standard, take heart from this story and the fact that God loves and 'rates' each one of us as unique individuals he made and cares about.

THEMES

Drugs
First impressions
Self-esteem

BIBLE REFERENCES

Psalms 30:6; 139
Job 30:1–15
Matthew 7:12; 19:19
Mark 12:31
Romans 12:3
1 Corinthians 3:16–17; 6:12–20
2 Corinthians 6:16
Galatians 6:3
Ephesians 2:22; 5:29
1 Timothy 4:4

22   Flying Ordeal

Just as TV newsreader Jonathan Hill was saying goodnight to viewers at the end of his bulletin, a housefly flew straight into his mouth. The shocked presenter was then faced with an awful dilemma. Like anyone, his instinct was to spit the insect out, but he knew that would disgust the TV viewers at home. So, with consummate professionalism, the 28-year-old swallowed hard and carried on as if nothing had happened!

Afterwards, Mr Hill told of his dilemma while reading the *Wales Tonight* news at the HTV studio in Cardiff. He said: 'I've faced some ordeals in front of the cameras, but nothing as bad as swallowing a fly. I opened my mouth to say "Goodnight" and it just zipped in.

'I choked on my words but just couldn't spit it out on camera. It's a teatime show and it might have made viewers ill. I had to be professional with so many people watching. There was only one choice: I had to grin and bear it. But the fly put up a good fight as it went down. I could feel it buzzing in my throat and I almost choked.'

His TV presenter colleague Lucy Cohen said: 'I could hear him coughing and choking. I thought he had a frog in his throat. When the lights went down he shot his hand out for a glass of water and gulped it down in one.

'It was then that he blurted out: "I've just swallowed a fly." I couldn't believe my ears – what a nightmare. I don't think I could have handled it as professionally as he did. I would probably have fainted on the spot.'

Hundreds of viewers phoned the studios after the broadcast to say they had seen Mr Hill swallow a fly.

'It will take me ages to live this one down,' said Mr Hill. 'Everyone has been joking with me and saying the rhyme about the old woman who swallowed a fly. It wasn't very nice, but I'm sure I won't die.'

His boss said: 'Jonathan was very professional and deserves a pat on the back. From now on we will be investing in a can of fly spray for the studio!'

But what made the incident an even greater sacrifice was the fact that Mr Hill is a dedicated vegetarian – it was the first meat he had tasted in years!

APPLICATION

Think of a time when you have been surprised by something and had to make an instant decision. Was the choice you made a good or bad one?

If you dropped a brick on your foot, what would come out of your mouth? Would you swear, or manage to confine yourself to a loud 'Ow!'?

'When we find ourselves in a difficult and dangerous situation, or are faced by a sudden dilemma requiring an instant decision, we find out about our true character, and the characters of others around us.' Do you agree or disagree with this statement?

THEMES

Determination
Dilemma
Perseverance
Self-control
Surprise
Swearing

BIBLE REFERENCES

Romans 5:3
Galatians 5:22
James 5:12
1 Peter 5:8

23 Foolish Flush

A mad-keen DIY enthusiast from Italy decided to install a toilet with a difference in his house. As well as enjoying DIY, 35-year-old Marcelos Cuban from Genoa was an avid collector of Roman antiquities, and his new loo was to be a combination of his two great hobbies. He designed the toilet himself, and converted a Roman sarcophagus (stone coffin) to use as a cistern. It had a Latin inscription on the side and, as it was made of stone, was very heavy.

Mr Cuban attached the cistern to the wall above his toilet before sitting down to try out his new loo. When he had finished, he reached up to pull the chain, only for the sarcophagus to rip from its mountings and fall onto his head, killing him instantly.

His shocked and mournful wife told reporters that she'd had the Latin inscription translated. It read: 'Good things always come from above.'

APPLICATION

Human folly and a lack of wisdom is a regular theme throughout the Bible – there is even a whole book (Proverbs) given over to it.

What other examples of foolishness (like trying to fix a large block of stone above your toilet seat) have you come across lately?

What are some of the characteristics of fools? The Bible lists the following:

- They are dishonest (Jeremiah 17:11)
- They are quick to express their anger (Proverbs 29:11)
- They despise discipline (Ezekiel 3:7)
- They say foolish things (Proverbs 18:6)
- They criticise and slander other people (2 Peter 2:11)
- They like arguments (1 Timothy 1:4)
- They promise much but deliver little (James 2:20)
- They trust in wealth not in God (Luke 12:16–21)

Acting foolishly is often treated light-heartedly. However, it is also a serious business! Although funny, the consequences of his lack of wisdom cost the DIY enthusiast his life. Proverbs 1:32 says: 'The waywardness of the simple will kill them, and the complacency of fools will destroy them.'

THEMES

DIY
Foolishness

BIBLE REFERENCES

Matthew 5:22; 7:24–27; 23:16–17; 25:1–13
Luke 11:39–40; 12:16–21; 24:25

24 Freeze Your Head?

A 47-year-old American suffering from a brain tumour wanted to put his head into cold storage for 500 years until a cure came along.

Tom Donaldson, a computer engineer with a PhD in physics, told newspaper reporters he also plans to freeze his cat and wife in suspended animation. Cryonics is the science of freezing people – or just their heads – in liquid nitrogen after their death, in the hope that one day they can be thawed out and cured of what killed them. Legal in America, there are already scores of complete bodies and heads in US laboratories.

However, Donaldson wants to be alive when they cut off his head so that his brain can be frozen before it begins to deteriorate. 'I am my brain, and if that goes, there's really not much hope of reanimating me in the future,' says Donaldson.

Cryonic scientists say there is no guarantee he can be revived from suspension. But Donaldson argues, 'I've got more hope than if they put me in the ground and I turn to dust, don't I?'

APPLICATION

If you had an inoperable brain tumour, would you consider cryonic suspension?

If you could say one thing to Tom Donaldson about his quest for immortality, what would it be?

Does death scare you? If science could extend your life span, how long would you like to live?

Romans 6:23 says: 'The wages of sin is death.' If Donaldson's plan is successful, will he escape from 'the wages of sin'?

THEMES

Death
Hope
Immortality
Life
Resurrection

BIBLE REFERENCES

Genesis 2:17; 3:19; 6:3; 25:8; 35:29
Job 7:6; 8:9; 9:25; 14:5; 16:22; 21:23–26; 38:17
Psalms 39:5; 71:5; 89:48; 102:11; 104:29; 115:17
Ecclesiastes 3:18–21
Isaiah 25:8; 40:6
Hosea 13:14
Luke 23:43
John 8:21, 24, 51; 11:23
Acts 2:26–27; 23:6
Romans 5:12; 6:23; 8:36; 14:8
1 Corinthians 15:24–26
Colossians 1:4–5
1 Timothy 6:7
2 Timothy 1:10
Titus 1:2
Hebrews 2:14–15; 9:27; 11:13, 21–22
James 4:14
2 Peter 1:13–14
Revelation 1:18; 2:11; 20:14; 21:4

25   Fruit and Nut Case

When Merryl Baker discovered three teeth in a nut and raisin chocolate bar she was shocked and horrified. Not surprisingly she complained to the manufacturers, and her story was repeated in the *Daily Star* newspaper. However, when some weeks later she visited the dentist, Ms Baker was told that three of her back teeth were missing. 'It was my mistake,' she said, 'and I feel such a fool.' Source: Retail Newsagent

APPLICATION

We all make mistakes. What has been your most embarrassing mistake? Some mistakes are more costly than others.

Discuss false accusations, for example Eli and Hannah (1 Samuel 1:14).

THEMES

False accusations
Mistakes
Surprise

BIBLE REFERENCES

Matthew 5:11
James 3:2

26 Full of Fear

Are you arachnophobic? Bridegroom-to-be Len Nupples of Montana woke on his wedding day morning to discover he was covered in dozens of highly poisonous black widow spiders. The 25-year-old was so terrified that he couldn't move or call out for help, as he thought that the slightest noise or movement would result in scores of bites and a painful death.

The hour of his wedding came and went. He ignored the frequent phone calls and the eventual hammering of his bride at the front door. Finally he was rescued by police who broke down the door to discover the frozen-in-fear man. It was then that it emerged that the spiders were plastic, stuck on by friends as a stag-night prank!

APPLICATION

What are you afraid of? Did you have any childhood fears which you overcame as you matured? Most children are afraid of the dark, as are some adults. The range of fears and phobias is huge.

Some fears can paralyse and inhibit our life – like the unfortunate Mr Nupples who missed out on his wedding day because of his fear of spiders. Have you got some fears or worries that you would like to be rid of? The psalmist wrote of how trusting in God helped him overcome the fear of passing through the valley of the shadow of death (Psalm 23). The Bible has many references to how we can overcome our fears if we have a relationship with God – our Protector and Shepherd.

THEMES

Fear
Phobias

BIBLE REFERENCES

Genesis 26:24; 35:17; 43:23; 50:19
Joshua 1:9; 8:1; 10:25
1 Samuel 4:20
2 Samuel 9:7
Psalm 23
Isaiah 7:4; 41:10; 43:5
Jeremiah 30:10; 42:11; 46:28
Daniel 10:12
Matthew 14:27; 17:7; 24:6; 28:5
Mark 5:36; 6:50
Luke 1:13; 2:10; 5:10; 8:50; 12:32
John 6:20; 14:27
Acts 18:9–10
Revelation 1:17

27 Good News

'Eureka! We've done it!' shouted two men in Berlin in 1815. These two men, Stolzel and Bluhmel, invented the valve which enables the player of a brass instrument (such as a trumpet) to momentarily add to the length of the tube in order to lower the pitch. As the valve is depressed by the finger, it deflects the air flow through a small loop of tubing, which alters the tone. This invention revolutionised brass musical instruments, giving them a far greater range.

The musical world owes a great debt to Stolzel and Bluhmel. Over the years hundreds of men and women have made inventions and discoveries which have changed our lives: mechanical devices like the telephone and medicines like penicillin.

But what would have happened if, for example, when Alexander Fleming discovered penicillin, he had thought to himself: 'This drug could save millions of lives but I am going to keep it a secret. I won't tell anyone about it'? I'm sure that you would agree with me that this would have been a very selfish act. Happily for all of us, penicillin was written about, tested and then became widely used. As a result, millions of people have avoided pain, suffering and death because Fleming shared his discovery.

In the same way, those of us who are Christians have a responsibility to share the good news of the gospel with other people. Having received the benefit of forgiveness of sins and a relationship with God, we must not keep silent but tell the world about Jesus Christ.

APPLICATION

Have you ever faced opposition or embarrassment for witnessing? Jesus said: 'If anyone is ashamed of me and my words, the Son of Man will be ashamed of him when he comes in his glory and in the glory of the Father and of the holy angels' (Luke 9:26).

THEMES

Discovery
Evangelism
Testimony
Witness

BIBLE REFERENCES

Matthew 10:18; 24:14
John 1:7, 32; 3:16; 5:33–34; 10:25; 19:35
Acts 1:8; 5:32
Romans 1:16; 8:16; 9:1
2 Timothy 1:8, 12
Hebrews 12:1
1 John 5:7–8

11/17 Pm

28   Gracious Gift

A woman walking in a park in the American town of Sante Fe came across an envelope on a park bench. The delighted woman found $100 inside and a handwritten note saying: 'Hello. Yes, this is for you. Money comes into my life and I am grateful for it. This is my way to express my gratitude. We live in an infinitely abundant universe. There is much more than enough for all of us. Enjoy! A friend.'

APPLICATION

'Be thankful for the smallest blessing, and you will deserve to receive greater' (Thomas à Kempis).

Sometimes we only really appreciate something when we lose it. Good health, clothes, a home, a job, a wife/husband/ children/family/boyfriend/girlfriend, friends, food, peace, warmth – all these things, and more, we tend to take for granted. It is right and important to be thankful to God for them. Counting our blessings will make us less greedy and more grateful for what we have. The secret of happiness is contentment rather than the accumulation of more wealth, fame or possessions.

THEMES

Generosity
Thankfulness

BIBLE REFERENCES

1 Chronicles 16:4, 8, 34; 23:30
Psalms 9:1; 18:49; 35:18; 69:30–31; 75:1; 86:12; 92:1; 95:2; 97:12; 100:4; 105:1; 107:1, 8, 15, 21, 31; 108:3; 111:1; 116:17; 118:1, 21, 29; 119:7; 136:1–3; 138:1; 139:14; 140:13; 145:10
Jonah 2:9
Luke 17:16; 22:17
Acts 27:35
Ephesians 5:4
Philippians 4:6
Colossians 2:7; 3:15; 4:2
1 Thessalonians 5:18
Hebrews 12:28; 13:15

29   Grand Exit

The final resting place of Sonny Bono has disappointed his former wife Cher. After visiting his grave in Palm Springs the singer announced that it did not 'reflect the fun and excitement he generated in life', and that she hopes to buy a more appropriate headstone and have it erected. 'A pinball machine or something like that . . . Sonny would dig it,' she said.

APPLICATION

When you die, how would you like people to remember you? What would be an appropriate epitaph? Proverbs tells us: 'The memory of the righteous is a blessing.'

The funeral of a Christian is markedly different from that of an atheist. Although there will still be some sadness and tears shed, there is also comfort and joy that the deceased is safe in the arms of Christ, and that one day we shall see them again.

'I don't mind dying – I just don't want to be there when it happens' (Woody Allen).

THEMES

Death
Funerals
Remembrance

BIBLE REFERENCES

Numbers 10:9
Ruth 1:17
Psalm 112:6
Proverbs 10:7
Ecclesiastes 6:3
Jeremiah 16:4
Matthew 26:13

The burial of famous biblical characters:

- Aaron – Deuteronomy 10:6
- Abraham – Genesis 25:9
- Absalom – 2 Samuel 18:17
- Ananias – Acts 5:6
- David – 1 Kings 2:10; Acts 2:29
- Deborah – Genesis 35:8
- Elisha – 2 Kings 13:20
- Gideon – Judges 8:32
- Hezekiah – 2 Chronicles 32:33
- Isaac – Genesis 35:29
- Jacob – Genesis 50:13
- Jehoshaphat – 1 Kings 22:50; 2 Chronicles 21:1
- Jephthah – Judges 12:7
- Jesus – Matthew 27:60; Mark 15:46; Luke 23:53; John 19:42; 1 Corinthians 15:4

- John the Baptist – Matthew 14:12; Mark 6:29
- Joseph – Joshua 24:32
- Joshua – Joshua 24:30; Judges 2:9
- Josiah – 2 Kings 23:30; 2 Chronicles 35:24
- Manasseh – 2 Kings 21:18; 2 Chronicles 33:20
- Moses – Deuteronomy 34:6
- Rachel – Genesis 35:19; 48:7
- Samson – Judges 16:31
- Samuel – 1 Samuel 25:1; 28:3
- Sapphira – Acts 5:10
- Saul – 1 Samuel 31:11–13
- Solomon – 1 Kings 11:43
- Stephen – Acts 8:2

30 Grave Report

Australian Paul Miller couldn't understand why his friends kept rushing up to hug him in the street, until they explained that they had read of his death in the local paper. When he bought a copy of the *Newcastle Herald* he found a death notice which read: 'Miller, Paul Leslie. Will be a much missed father, grandfather and friend.'

His son Jason had placed the notice so that he could get off work to go whelk fishing. 'The advert cost him $16.80, but he showed it to his boss and was given seven days' bereavement leave,' said the angry Miller Senior.

APPLICATION

'Food gained by fraud tastes sweet to a man, but he ends up with a mouth full of gravel' (Proverbs 20:17).

Deceit goes right back to the beginning – when Satan deceived Eve (Genesis 3:13) – and will go on to the end of the world. Revelation predicts that Satan will deceive the whole world in the 'end times' (20:8). Two of Satan's own names are 'deceiver' and 'father of lies'.

Biblical stories of deception:

- Jacob deceived Isaac – Genesis 27:11–24, 35

- Jacob deceived Laban – Genesis 31:20

- Jacob was deceived over Rachel – Genesis 29:25

- Jacob's sons deceived the men of Shechem – Genesis 34:13

- Pharaoh acted deceitfully – Exodus 8:29
- Michal deceived her father – 1 Samuel 19:13,17
- Ziba deceived Mephibosheth – 2 Samuel 19:26
- The Magi deceived Herod – Matthew 2:16

THEMES

Death
Deception
Lies

BIBLE REFERENCES

Genesis 3:13
Deuteronomy 11:16
Psalms 10:7; 32:2; 34:13; 35:20; 36:3; 52:4; 101:7
Proverbs 4:24; 20:17; 24:28; 30:8
Jeremiah 9:8; 17:9; 37:9; 49:16
Matthew 13:22; 24:11
Mark 4:9; 7:20–22; 13:5
John 8:44
Acts 13:10
Romans 1:29; 3:13; 7:11; 16:18
1 Corinthians 3:18
2 Corinthians 11:3
Galatians 6:3
Ephesians 5:6
Colossians 2:8
2 Thessalonians 2:3
1 Timothy 2:14; 4:1
2 Timothy 3:13
Hebrews 3:13
James 1:16, 22, 26

1 Peter 2:1; 3:10
1 John 1:6–8; 3:7; 4:20
2 John 7
Revelation 12:9; 20:7–8; 21:8; 22:15

31 Hard-Hitting Warning

Children as young as nine have been shown a video which depicts the painful death of a heroin addict in an attempt to warn them away from drugs.

The hard-hitting video has been shown in primary schools in the Rhondda Valley, south Wales, where there were eighteen heroin-related deaths between 1997 and 1999. The video, entitled *The Trap*, was filmed in the Rhondda and features the story of a heroin addict. In one graphic scene the addict injects himself, then sinks to his knees and dies in a rubbish-strewn subway. The next scene shows a coffin being lowered into a grave.

A 20-year-old local heroin addict plays the lead role. He took part in the project because he wanted to warn children about the dangers of hard drugs.

Inspector Paul Cannon said that police had co-operated because five years of anti-drugs campaigns had failed.

APPLICATION

What are the main reasons why people take drugs? Have any of the anti-drugs campaigns changed the way you think about drugs? What do you think of this video idea?

If you were an advisor to the government on reducing the number of young people who take illegal drugs, what would your message/advice be?

Heroin, cocaine and marijuana do not get a mention in the Bible because at the time they were not known. However, the Bible does warn against intoxication and drunkenness. Why do you think God forbids this?

THEMES

Drugs
Drunkenness
Warnings

BIBLE REFERENCES

Proverbs 23:21
1 Corinthians 6:10, 19
Galatians 5:21
Ephesians 5:18
1 Timothy 3:3
Titus 1:7
1 Peter 4:3

32   Henry and the Flood

There was a man called Henry who lived near a river. Henry was a very religious man. One day, the river rose over the banks and flooded the town, and Henry was forced to climb onto his porch roof.

While sitting there, a man in a boat came along and told Henry to get in the boat with him. Henry replied, 'No, that's OK, God will take care of me.' So the man in the boat rowed away.

The water rose and Henry climbed onto his roof. Then another boat came along and the person in that one told Henry to get in. Henry replied, 'No, that's OK, God will take care of me.' The person in the boat went away.

The water rose even higher, and Henry climbed onto his chimney. Then a helicopter came along, and a woman operating the winch in the helicopter told Henry to catch hold of the harness they were about to drop to him. Henry called to her, 'That's OK.'

The woman said, 'Are you sure?'

Henry replied, 'Yeah, I'm sure God will take care of me.'

Eventually, the water rose even higher and Henry drowned. When Henry got up to heaven's gates and met St Peter, he said to the saint, 'I thought you guys would take care of me! What happened?'

St Peter sighed and answered, 'Well, we sent you two boats and a helicopter. What else did you want?'

APPLICATION

Some people, like Henry, don't seem to recognise an answer to prayer when it bites them on the nose! God can use circumstances, modern technology, other people (not necessarily Christians) and a host of other things to answer our prayers and meet our needs – it doesn't always require a miracle, an angelic visit, or the words or work of a Christian.

'Foolish people lack judgement and fail to discern God's purpose and truth' (*NIV Thematic Study Bible* notes on 'discernment').

THEMES

Discernment
Prayer
Warnings

BIBLE REFERENCES

Deuteronomy 1:39; 32:28
Psalm 91:14–16
Isaiah 7:15–16
Daniel 2:21
Matthew 7:7–11

33 Hold the Line

A manager of a concert hall was telephoned by a woman who told him that she had lost an expensive diamond brooch during a performance there the previous night.

'Have you found my diamond brooch?' she asked.

'No madam, but we will look for it now,' replied the manager. 'Please hold the line.'

During a quick search the valuable gem was found. When the manager returned to the phone, however, he discovered the lady had hung up. She never called back, so the expensive jewellery went unclaimed.

APPLICATION

Prayer often requires perseverance. When Jesus was in the Garden of Gethsemane he asked his disciples to pray, but they fell asleep. Describe any prayers that you have made that are apparently unanswered.

THEMES

Lost and found
Patience
Perseverance

BIBLE REFERENCES

Matthew 7:7
Luke 18:1–7
Ephesians 6:18
1 Thessalonians 5:17
Hebrews 12:1

34 Hot Lips

It's strange but true – a man once got frozen to his car!

On a particularly cold winter morning in Lancashire a man discovered he couldn't get his car key to work properly in the lock on the door because it was iced up. In an attempt to melt the ice he crouched down and began blowing warm air onto the door lock. After thirty seconds or so he realised that his lips had become frozen to the lock!

While he was in this crouching position an old lady passed by. The man tried to alert her to his distress, but he could only manage a muffled 'Urghh!'. Alarmed, she hurried away.

It was a full twenty minutes before his constant hot breathing brought his freedom. He subsequently received the nickname 'hot lips' from friends and family.

APPLICATION

When Jesus was on earth, much of what he said and did could be described as 'strange but true'. He was out of the ordinary and he changed people's lives radically.

Tell the group about a 'strange but true' or embarrassing experience you have had.

THEMES

Embarrassment
Misunderstanding

BIBLE REFERENCES

Numbers 22:28
Judges 12:6
Job 16:3
Psalms 45:1; 141:3
Proverbs 13:3; 18:21
Ecclesiastes 3:7; 5:3; 6:11; 10:14
Matthew 6:7; 23:3; 26:73
Mark 7:32
Luke 1:64
John 10:27

35 Honest Henry

When Henry Snowdown ordered a flame-grilled burger and chips at Burger King, he was mistakenly handed $4,000 in used dollar notes in a paper bag. The staff at the Florida burger branch had been ordered to keep their takings in the paper bags to outwit robbers.

Honest Henry handed back the money saying: 'I was glad I was able to do the right thing.'

APPLICATION

What would you have done? Kept the money (over £2,000) or handed it back? Think of a time when you have been given money by mistake – perhaps it was extra change at a shop. What did you do, and how did you feel about your actions afterwards?

A proverb says: 'Honesty is the best policy.' Is that always true? The dictionary defines honesty as fair, righteous and truthful in speech and act, not lying, cheating or stealing, being truly sincere. These qualities describe God's own nature and they are required of all those who follow Christ.

THEMES

Honesty
Stealing

BIBLE REFERENCES

Exodus 18:21
2 Samuel 7:28
Psalms 15:1–2; 19:7
Proverbs 29:10
Matthew 22:16
Romans 1:18
2 Corinthians 4:2
Ephesians 4:15
Philippians 4:8
1 Timothy 3:8
Titus 1:7; 2:7–8
1 Peter 2:22

36   Just the Job

After nearly 3,000 rejections in thirteen years of job hunting, Graham Hoskins finally succeeded in 1998 and started work as a valet with a car and van hire company. The 50-year-old bachelor had attended hundreds of interviews in his quest to get off the dole, but they only resulted in a growing pile of rejection letters.

'I never gave up hope, and now I can't believe I'm finally going back to work,' said a delighted Mr Hoskins before his first day at work.

Living in a south Wales unemployment black spot, he struggled to make ends meet and maintain his sense of dignity. Now he is happily cleaning vans and has doubled his income, thanks to his new job.

Mr Hoskins was made redundant from his last job at a factory in 1984, and joined a Jobseekers' Club in 1987. He was on its books longer than anyone else. Over the years he kept files on all the jobs he applied for, but after reaching his fiftieth birthday, he feared he would never work again.

'I just kept getting rejections; it was really disheartening,' he recalled. 'Now I feel I can look forward to the year ahead.'

APPLICATION

Do you think you would have continued to make every attempt to get a job after thirteen years and nearly 3,000 snubs?

What makes some people so determined, when others would give up more quickly? What examples of perseverance despite the odds can you think of?

'In the factory we manufacture cosmetics, in the store we sell hope' (Charles Revlon, cosmetics manufacturer).

THEMES

Determination
Failure
Hope
Perseverance

BIBLE REFERENCES

Ruth 1:12
2 Kings 4:28
Proverbs 19:18
Ecclesiastes 9:4
Acts 11:23; 13:43
Romans 5:3–4; 11:14; 12:12
1 Corinthians 13:7; 15:58; 16:13
2 Corinthians 1:21–22; 12:12
Philippians 1:27
Colossians 1:4–5, 27
1 Thessalonians 2:19; 5:8
2 Timothy 1:13; 4:8
Titus 2:13
Hebrews 2:1; 3:6; 4:14; 10:23
James 1:4
1 Peter 3:15
2 Peter 1:5–8
Revelation 3:11

37   Kiss and Make Up

During a crucial World Cup football game, England's David Beckham was sent off for kicking Argentina's Diego Simeone in retaliation for a foul moments earlier. The referee didn't hesitate to show Beckham the red card, leaving England one man short for the rest of the game. England eventually lost the game in a penalty shoot-out and was eliminated from the competition. Many English football supporters blamed Beckham for England's exit. The Manchester United star then suffered a torrid time being booed by opposition fans, and received a barrage of abuse for several months playing at away club stadiums across the country.

Less than a year later, Beckham was to face Simeone in a club game when Manchester United played Inter Milan in the quarter finals of the European Champions' Cup. Before the game Simeone told the press that he had fallen over when Beckham kicked him, to ensure Beckham got the red card.

Despite this, at the final whistle, Beckham approached Simeone, shook hands, embraced and swapped shirts. It later emerged that David Beckham's mother, Sandra, suggested he swapped shirts with Simeone.

Afterwards Beckham told reporters: 'I hope that my gesture ends it all. There was a lot of hype before the game about Simeone and myself, but it's all in the past now.'

APPLICATION

If you were in David Beckham's boots, would you have done the same thing? Or would you have kept the feud alive by trying to fake a fall and getting your own back?

Forgiving someone who has done you a wrong is often difficult, but the Bible teaches that it is vital we do this if we want God to forgive us for our own wrongdoing.

What was the best piece of advice your mother gave you?

THEMES

Forgiveness
Parents
Sport

BIBLE REFERENCES

Exodus 34:5–7
Numbers 14:18
2 Chronicles 7:14
Psalms 32:1–5; 51:1–2
Isaiah 43:25; 55:6–7
Jeremiah 31:31–34
Matthew 18:23–35; 26:27–28
Mark 2:5–7
Luke 6:37; 7:36–50; 11:4; 15:11–32; 17:3–4; 23:33–34
John 1:29; 8:3–11; 20:21–23
Acts 7:59–60
Romans 3:23
2 Corinthians 5:11
Ephesians 4:32
Colossians 3:12–13
Hebrews 8:8–12
James 5:13–16
1 Peter 3:8–9
1 John 1:8–9

38   Life-Saving Legacy

6.30
5/02

A father who had been waiting years for a heart transplant finally got one – from his daughter.

Chester Szuber, 58, was given his new chance of life after 22-year-old Patti died in a car crash. Patti's family rushed to her side after the accident in Knocksville, Tennessee, left her in a critical condition. Doctors were unable to save her, but discovered she was carrying a donor card.

Her brother, Bob, told journalists: 'We all felt that an organ donation was exactly what Patti would have wanted. At the time we had no idea that the donation of Patti's heart to our father was even a possibility.'

Chester had been waiting for a donor for four years, and the family immediately contacted their own doctor who confirmed that the heart was compatible.

'After discussion involving the entire family, we decided the donation of her heart to her father was what Patti would have wanted beyond a shadow of a doubt,' said Bob.

APPLICATION

We are saved because Christ shed his blood and became our substitute, taking on himself our punishment, so that through his death we can have life.

THEMES

Blood donors
Character of God

Inheritance
Legacy
Life-saver
Transplants

BIBLE REFERENCES

Genesis 9:4–6
Exodus 12:7–13, 22–23
Leviticus 17:11
Psalms 2:8; 37:18; 61:5; 65:5–8; 89:26
Isaiah 9:6
Matthew 5:5; 6:9; 23:9; 25:34
Mark 10:17; 14:24
Luke 10:25
John 6:53–55; 8:41–42
Acts 20:32; 26:18
1 Corinthians 10:16
2 Corinthians 6:18
Ephesians 1:7; 2:13
Colossians 1:12
1 Peter 1:18–19
Revelation 1:5; 12:11

39   Lucky Catch   w/c 6/03

Baseball fan Philip Ozersky was sitting in the stands watching a game when star hitter Mark McGwire smashed the ball up into the crowd for a home run, straight into Philip's outstretched hands.

That catch earned 26-year-old Philip a fortune! Under baseball rules, the ball became his to keep, but it wasn't just any home run hit he had caught. McGwire's swipe for the St Louis Cardinals was a record-breaking seventieth home run in one season, breaking the previous record which dated back to the 1960s.

The five ounces of yarn and cowhide which cost just £3 was auctioned a few months later in January 1999, for a staggering £1.9 million! The sale in New York became a battle between a clothing tycoon and an anonymous telephone bidder, both of whom wanted the record-breaking ball. Eventually the telephone bidder won, having bid $3 million. The baseball sold for six times more than the record for any other sports artefact.

Philip said after the auction: 'It's been the most exciting time of my life. Here I am, just an ordinary baseball fan, and all of a sudden I catch a piece of history.'

He added: 'I just went with my friends to see a game and drink some beer. It's pretty amazing to me. I'd never caught a home run ball before. I took the ball around town for a few days and slept with it next to my bed.'

In the space of a few seconds the lucky catch meant that Philip swapped his modest lifestyle for a fortune.

APPLICATION

What's the most surprising/unexpected/fortunate thing that's ever happened to you?

The Bible has many surprising stories of the unexpected: Jephthah made a rash promise to sacrifice to God the first living thing which greeted him on his victorious return from battle – this turned out to be his daughter (Judges 11).

The Bible teaches that many people will be surprised by the unexpected return of Christ.

THEMES

Luck
Second Coming of Christ
Surprise
Unexpected

BIBLE REFERENCES

Matthew 24:37–44, 50
Luke 12:40–46; 21:34–35

40   Men Behaving Badly

Ganwars 30/3/03

One woman is so disillusioned with men that she has decided to marry a tree instead!

Environmentalist Dee Brophy has 'fallen for' and announced herself 'engaged to' a silver birch near her south London home. Her only problem has been getting a vicar to agree to carry out the ceremony. 'This tree will be more loyal and affectionate than some guys I've dated,' she sadly declared.

A lady from Germany has a similarly negative view of men. The 35-year-old from Hamburg couldn't understand why strange men kept phoning her up and asking her out on dates. Eventually her husband confessed that he had placed a lonely hearts advert in a magazine because he was leaving her and didn't want her to be on her own at Christmas!

APPLICATION

Many people have been disappointed in love. If you have been let down or even betrayed – maybe more than once – it can become very hard to move on without allowing the disappointment to turn to bitterness that can spoil your life. Some men and women regard the opposite sex as 'the enemy' because of the wrongs that have been committed against them. However, instead of moving on they regard all men/women as the same, and the main casualty in all this is themselves.

To forgive and forget is often very difficult, but the Bible teaches that our own forgiveness by God depends on us forgiving those who have sinned against us.

THEMES

Disappointment
Forgiveness
Opposite sex

BIBLE REFERENCES

Proverbs 17:9
Matthew 6:14–15; 18:21–22, 35
Mark 11:25
Luke 6:37; 7:42; 11:4; 17:3–4
2 Corinthians 2:7, 10
Ephesians 4:32
Colossians 3:13

41   Imagine a £10 Million Inheritance!

Imagine inheriting a house worth £10 million. How would you feel?

That dream became a reality for one 15-year-old lad in 1993 when out of the blue he inherited a country manor house, complete with his own butler!

Simon Cunliffe-Lister discovered he was the beneficiary of the will of a distant cousin, who had no children of his own. In his will, he left Simon the historic Burton Agnes Hall, worth £10 million, plus forty-two acres of land. Simon was instantly able to lord it over the elegant Elizabethan house, which had valuable Renoir and Gauguin paintings on its panelled walls.

Simon, whose interests included watching the TV soap *Neighbours* and playing in a rock band, initially considered using the house for a rave, but then accepted this was out of the question.

His girlfriend told Simon she loved the house. 'I suppose most women would be impressed,' he said. 'I'll have to keep an eye out for gold-diggers.'

APPLICATION

What would you do with £10 million?

Some people think that a lot of money would remove every problem from their lives. Simon said he would have to look out for gold-diggers. What other disadvantages or problems do you think he and other very rich people face?

'The way people use their money reveals where their priorities lie.' Do you agree with this statement?

THEMES

Luck
Money
Priorities

BIBLE REFERENCES

Psalm 62:10
Proverbs 22:1
Matthew 6:24–34
Luke 12:13–34
1 Timothy 3:3
Hebrews 13:5
James 5:1–6

42   It's Simply Not Cricket!

It was an idyllic English country Sunday afternoon scene. The sun was shining, and the gentle sound of bees buzzing in flowers, the chinking of tea cups and the thud of cricket bat on ball filled the air. But suddenly all that changed.

Just as the bowler for the Dorchester 3rd XI was about to begin his run up towards the wicket, the fielders and batsmen turned in astonishment as a car roared across the pitch. Like a scene from a TV sitcom, players scattered. The car skidded to a shuddering halt as the woman at the wheel hurled some keys and a few angry words at an embarrassed fielder.

Mother-of-two Jennifer Christian then got out of the car and walked off the field. Her husband Eric, the cricket club treasurer, got in the car and gingerly drove off.

Later Mrs Christian explained that she was angry because her husband had told her the cricket was cancelled and he had offered to look after the children all afternoon. She later discovered the match was back on and her husband had disappeared, leaving her with the kids. In a rage she decided to take action!

APPLICATION

Have you got a hot temper? Has it ever got you into trouble?

Some people bottle up their emotions and then explode in frustration instead of calmly dealing with conflict, while others sulk, cry or shout and scream. What did you think of the actions of the man and his wife? What would have been a better way of dealing with the conflict?

THEMES

Communication
Conflict
Marriage
Temper

BIBLE REFERENCES

Proverbs 14:17, 29; 15:18; 16:32; 17:27; 19:19; 22:24; 29:22
1 Corinthians 7:28
Titus 1:7

43   I Wish I Was Dead

Despite having a loving girlfriend and being successful in his studies, Craig Wilson killed himself. The 18-year-old from Manchester lay down on a railway track and was decapitated by a passing passenger train.

Inches away from his body was his last weary comment on his life, spelled out in railway ballast stone: 'BORED'. His diary was also found near his body. The last entry read: 'Time to die . . . cremate me and put my ashes in the North Stand end goal mouth (Manchester City Football Club).'

His father told an inquest that neither the local high school, which Craig left at sixteen with excellent GCSE grades, nor a computer course at college had provided enough challenge for him.

Craig often complained to friends, 'I'm bored.' After drinking four pints of lager and complaining that he could still 'taste life', he went off and killed himself.

APPLICATION

What makes life worth living for you? Is suicide a brave or cowardly act?

If you had met Craig on the way to the railway, what would you have said to him to try to persuade him not to kill himself?

Most Christians believe that life is a gift from God and that it is not for us to destroy our own life deliberately. Suicide is a sin against God who created life and is a rejection of his sovereignty. It is an act of despair and prematurely deprives one's family and society of a member. Some churches withhold 'Christian burial' on church-owned burial plots for those who kill themselves.

In his letter to the Galatians, Paul writes that Jesus understands our reality. He has been through testing and temptation and has experienced everything that affects us, except that he didn't sin. Since we have this Friend and Priest who gives us access to God the Father, let's talk to him and receive the mercy and help he can provide.

THEMES

Boredom
Suicide

BIBLE REFERENCES

1 Samuel 31:4
2 Samuel 17:23
1 Kings 16:18
Matthew 27:5
Acts 1:18
Galatians 4:14–16

44 Lifesaver

5/02
6.30.

One minute he was trying to settle an argument between neighbours, the next he was running towards a toddler who was about to fall from a block of flats. It was just another routine shift for police constable Darius Hemmatpour. He had been called to intervene between two noisy neighbours arguing over a trivial matter. Suddenly, from the corner of his eye, he spotted a toddler clinging onto a swinging window frame above a thirty-foot drop.

As 21-month-old Kieran Holland struggled to hold on, the policeman ran towards the block of flats. The toddler lost his grip and fell onto a ledge, then fell further towards the concrete path below. Just in time PC Hemmatpour arrived and half caught the toddler, breaking his fall.

Kieran sustained a fractured skull but subsequently made a full recovery. PC Hemmatpour told newspaper reporters: 'I'm just glad I was there. I've never been affected by anything so much in the six years I've been a policeman.'

Kieran's grandmother said: 'He is a hero and saved my grandson's life.'

APPLICATION

Close your eyes and imagine you are in the shoes of that policeman. Imagine the shock of seeing the child in danger and the suspense as you run to the spot, not knowing if you will reach the child in time. Then the agony and fear as the child falls and you look up and try to catch him. Now imagine the relief and happiness as the child, although injured, is safe, and you receive the grateful thanks of the family and the admiration of your colleagues and friends.

Now imagine something different. Picture yourself as a child aged nine, being told of the incident that happened when you were just a toddler. Imagine meeting the policeman and what you would want to say to him. Try to describe your feelings of gratitude towards this stranger whose actions saved your life.

The Bible teaches that Jesus Christ has saved you from an eternal death. Because of his willingness to die and receive the punishment for our sin, and because he came back to life, it is possible for us to receive forgiveness, become part of God's family and be saved from hell. We can look forward to eternal life in heaven, and a more fulfilled life on earth now.

THEMES

Gospel
Heroes
Life
Saviour
Thankfulness

BIBLE REFERENCES

Luke 1:46–49
John 3:16; 4:42; 10:15; 15:13
Acts 5:31
Ephesians 2:5, 8
2 Thessalonians 2:13
1 Timothy 1:15; 2:4; 4:10
James 1:21
Jude 25

45 Married Mishap

It was supposed to be the big day of his wedding, but it turned out to be the start of a very bad day instead.

As he walked into church, bridegroom Francesco Giaculli twisted his ankle. His best man carried him in, but hit his head on the door and dropped the unfortunate Francesco on his back. On the way to the hospital, the ambulance crashed, breaking Francesco's nose. When he finally got to the hospital, a screen fell on him and cut open his head.

Following this catalogue of disasters, bride Maria Bacchetti called off the wedding, declaring: 'I'd be mad to wed this accident-prone man.'

APPLICATION

Marriage is part of God's plan for the human race. It is the union of a man and a woman in a permanent life-long monogamous relationship, and a serious decision which should not be made lightly or without much thought and preparation.

Men and women are different, but the Bible teaches they have complementary roles. Their differences are not just biological, but they are emotionally and temperamentally different as well.

The relationship between a believer and God is sometimes likened to marriage in the Bible: for example Isaiah 54:5, the story of Hosea and his bride, and Christ returning for his bride the church in Revelation.

'Don't praise marriage on the third day, but after the third year' (Russian proverb).

Some notable marriages in the Bible:

- Isaac and Rebekah – Genesis 24:67

- Ahab and Jezebel – 1 Kings 16:31

- Joseph and Mary – Matthew 1:24

- Wedding at Cana – John 2:1

THEMES

Marriage
Commitment

BIBLE REFERENCES

Deuteronomy 24:5
Esther 1:17–20
Psalms 19:4–5; 128:3
Proverbs 5:15–20; 12:4; 18:22; 31:10–31
Isaiah 54:5; 62:4–5
Jeremiah 31:32
Hosea 2:16
Malachi 2:14–15
Matthew 22:2
1 Corinthians 7:3–5
2 Corinthians 11:2
Ephesians 5:22, 25
Colossians 3:18–19
Titus 2:4
1 Peter 3:1–7
Revelation 1:7–9; 21:2–9

46   Milan – Then Double Maths!

Having completed the photo shoot in Milan for a major advertising brand, British model Rosalind Halstead needed to use the phone before flying home. She called her mother – to ask her to iron her school uniform! The next day the 14-year-old was back studying for her GCSEs at school in London.

Rosalind is one of a growing number of schoolgirl models who skip off school for the fashion catwalks of Paris, Milan, New York and London.

Rosalind's school gave permission for her to take a week off. One fashion agency representative explains: 'School has to come first. We never mention a job without checking with a child's parents first. Imagine if we say, "Oh, here's a £40,000 job in Paris," and then Mum says, "Sorry, you've got too much homework."'

One former teen model, Maxine Henshilwood, says: 'At the age of twenty I was earning more than the average man in his fifties.'

Some fashion agencies are reluctant to take on under-17-year-olds, but the trend for using younger, thinner and even pre-pubescent girls has created a big demand for young teen talent.

Not all adults seem to have the interests of young models at heart. Fashion photographer Phillip Berryman cites the story of a casting for a nude advertising shoot. Among hundreds of hopefuls was a 13-year-old, chaperoned by her mother. Even though the agency knew about the nudity they still sent her, and both the girl and her mother said they had no problem with it. Source: *Times Educational Supplement*

APPLICATION

What are the implications – both helpful and harmful – of teens doing modelling?

In 1999 Kate Moss revealed that she had recently attended a clinic to help her overcome alcohol and drug problems. She claimed most models took illegal drugs and over-indulged in booze. Why do you think that is?

'Everyone has their price. If the money is good enough, no matter what you do, it softens any negative impact.' Do you agree or disagree with that statement?

If you could earn £30,000 for posing nude, would you do it?

THEMES

Ethics
Money
Motivation
Values

BIBLE REFERENCES

Deuteronomy 8:12–14, 18
Job 31:24, 28
Psalms 52:7; 62:10
Proverbs 11:4; 27:24
Ecclesiastes 5:10
Isaiah 10:3
Jeremiah 48:7
Matthew 6:24
Luke 8:14; 12:16–21; 16:13–14

Ephesians 5:5
1 Timothy 3:3, 8; 6:10, 17
2 Timothy 3:2
Titus 1:7
Hebrews 13:5
James 1:11; 5:1–3
1 Peter 5:2
Revelation 18:14

47   Miss Understanding

An 8-year-old girl went to her dad, who was working in the yard. She asked him, 'Daddy, what is sex?'

The father was surprised that she would ask such a question, but decided that if she was old enough to ask, then she was old enough to get a straight answer. He proceeded to tell her all about the 'birds and the bees'.

When he had finished explaining, the little girl was looking at him with her mouth hanging open. The father asked her, 'Why did you ask the question?'

The little girl replied, 'Mum told me to tell you that dinner would be ready in just a couple of secs.'

APPLICATION

It's easy to misunderstand something, especially if you mishear a conversation or comment. The slightest change of emphasis or punctuation can dramatically change the message received and understood.

The process of communication is fraught with difficulties, and misunderstandings often occur. What is the funniest or most dramatic example that's happened to you?

The book of Genesis (11:6–9) explains that once everyone spoke the same language, but due to people's pride and arrogance God introduced the confusion of lots of different languages. Ever since people have been struggling to understand each other!

THEMES

Communication
Misunderstanding
Surprise

BIBLE REFERENCES

Numbers 22:28
Judges 12:6
Job 16:3
Proverbs 13:3; 18:21
Psalms 45:1; 141:3
Ecclesiastes 3:7; 5:3; 6:11; 10:14
Matthew 6:7; 23:3; 26:73
Mark 7:32
Luke 1:64
John 10:27

48 Mobile Tomb

When 17-year-old Guy Akrish was killed in a road accident near his home in Israel, his family was shocked and grief-stricken. They had a family conference to decide on an appropriate memorial to Guy's short but vibrant life. Wherever Guy went in life it seemed as if his mobile phone had been glued to his ear, so when it came to choosing the tombstone, they all agreed it should be a marble mobile phone!

Now anyone who visits the cemetery in the southern town of Ashkelon can see the unusual tomb and read the epitaph on the headstone's digital display which reads: 'Hello, this is Guy. How are you doing?'

Guy's sister, Diana, said the family decided on the unique memorial 'because Guy so much enjoyed talking on the phone'.

APPLICATION

Although most tombstones are regular in shape, some people have more elaborate memorials. Highgate Cemetery in north London is famous for its unusual tombs. A grand piano, a faithful hound, pyramids and lions are just a few of the more unusual tombstones. If your friends/relatives were to choose an elaborate and unusual tombstone for you, what would best sum up your life?

Knowing that his followers might forget, Jesus used bread and wine to remind them of his body and blood which would be broken and shed. Communion is a memorial of

Christ's death and the new agreement between God and his
people.

THEMES

Communion
Memorials
Remembrance

BIBLE REFERENCES

Exodus 12:14; 28:12
Numbers 15:37–40; 16:39–40
Joshua 4:7; 24:27
Matthew 26:13
Luke 22:19

49   Nagging Wife

Tired of his wife's nagging, Hendrick Bengtsson, who is
deaf, tried to sever his wife's fingers because she nagged in
sign language!

Bengtsson, aged fifty-three, spoke to reporters from his
prison cell in Stockholm: 'I'd had enough. I would close my
eyes, but the moment I opened them she would start again.'

APPLICATION

What things irritate you most in life? What is there in your
own character or behaviour that annoys others?

THEMES

Nagging
Torment

BIBLE REFERENCES

Numbers 33:55
Joshua 23:13
Judges 16:16
Proverbs 30:21–23
Luke 8:28; 18:5

Trn Feb 11.

50 Name Again *16/17/01 Pm.*

An Australian woman was granted a divorce by a judge because she couldn't cope with being ridiculed about her name – Pauline Rottenbottom. She told the court that her husband's relatives had changed their name to Robottom but he refused to do so.

However, it appears she has not learned from the past, as she has announced plans to marry again. Her husband-to-be is Raymond Ticklemore!

APPLICATION

We all make mistakes. However, the wise person learns from their mistakes, while the fool commits the same mistake over and over again. What mistakes have you learned from? What mistakes have you made time and time again?

THEMES

Mistakes
Names

BIBLE REFERENCES

Genesis 2:19–20; 32:29
Judges 13:17
Isaiah 9:6
Jeremiah 23:6, 13
Micah 3:5

Matthew 1:21, 25; 2:23
Luke 1:31; 2:21
John 7:47
Acts 4:12
Philippians 2:9–10
James 3:2
2 Peter 3:17
Revelation 19:12

51   Not so Lucky!

A man punched a fortune-teller in the face when she forecast that he would soon be sent to prison. For assaulting the woman Peter Moore was duly sent to jail in Gary, Texas.

Another fortune-teller, Maria Tivoli of Verona, Italy, was less accurate. She is being sued after failing to predict that her crystal ball would fall off her balcony onto a passer-by's head!

Having a superstitious mother didn't help Giuseppe Platini of Bologna to pass his driving test. When his mother realised she hadn't wished him luck, she drove to the test centre but discovered her son had already left for the examination. Driving recklessly she caught up with him on a dual carriageway, where she pulled alongside and screamed, 'Good luck, my Giuseppe!'

Distracted, he lost control of the car and careered into a wall. The impact broke the examiner's legs.

APPLICATION

Do you avoid walking under ladders or crossing the path of a black cat? Letting superstitions rule your life or affect your actions shows you are not fully trusting in God. He knows the future and asks us to trust him for guidance and direction.

Attempts to discover the unknown or the future by supernatural means, involving the spirit world or by consulting fortune-tellers, is expressly forbidden in the Bible. According to the Bible, divination has disastrous consequences.

THEMES

Divination
Fortune-telling
Luck
Superstition

BIBLE REFERENCES

Exodus 7:11
Leviticus 19:31; 20:6
Numbers 22:6
Deuteronomy 18:9–12
2 Kings 9:22; 21:6
Isaiah 44:24–25
Zechariah 10:2
Acts 8:9–13; 13:6–9; 16:16–18
Galatians 5:19–21

52   One Wish

An 18-year-old lad was walking along Brighton beach when he stumbled across an old lamp. He picked it up and rubbed it and out popped a genie. The genie said, 'OK, so you released me from the lamp, but this is the fourth time this week and I'm getting a little sick of these wishes, so you can forget about three. You only get one wish.'

The young man sat and thought about it for a while and said, 'I've always wanted to go to America, but I'm too scared to fly and I get very seasick. So could you build me a bridge to America so I can drive over there?'

The genie laughed and replied, 'That's impossible. Think of the logistics of that. How would the supports ever reach the bottom of the Atlantic? Think of how much concrete . . . how much steel! No, think of another wish.'

The teenager agreed and tried to come up with a really good wish. He said, 'I've been out with three different girls in the past three years. My girlfriends have always said that I don't care and I'm insensitive. I wish I could understand women: to know what they are thinking when they give me the silent treatment; to know why they are crying; to know what they want when they say "nothing".'

The genie replied, 'Do you want that bridge to be two lanes or three?'

APPLICATION

What two things about the opposite sex do you like most and understand least?

When asked, one woman said that her new husband was perfect – except she wished he wouldn't leave the toilet seat up! What other irritating traits do men have in the eyes of women – and vice versa?

'The mystery and difference between the two sexes is part of what makes romance so exciting.' Discuss this statement.

THEMES

Gender
Misunderstanding
Sexuality
Stereotypes

BIBLE REFERENCES

Genesis 1:27; 2:21–23; 5:2
Matthew 19:4
Mark 10:6
1 Corinthians 11:9
Galatians 3:28

53   On Time – We Promise!

A train company with a notoriously poor record for delays and late arrivals promised its customers that it would achieve 100 per cent punctuality on its 'Performance Day'. But on the given day, passengers watched in amazement as the 6.20am train sailed through four stations without making its scheduled stops.

The company, which operates one of the busiest commuter lines in England, ordered staff to ensure all trains into the capital met punctuality targets that day. A spokesman for the train company explained that it was 'an operational decision' not to stop at four stations, to help the late train make up time. The company announced that as a result all but two of its 180 morning rush-hour trains had met the punctuality targets.

One angry commuter left standing on the platform said: 'We couldn't believe it. There's no point in running trains if you don't pick up passengers.'

Meanwhile, an American soft drinks company has made a different sort of promise to its customers. They have launched a new range of fizzy drinks called *Belchers*. They promise the drinker 'the loudest, longest and most explosive belches you've ever had'. The promised effect is achieved by including twice the usual amount of bubbles.

APPLICATION

Promises are easy to make but hard to keep! One of the most solemn promises that men and women can make is to 'remain faithful until death do us part' when they marry. Sadly, however, millions fail to keep their marriage vows, and divorce, with bitter consequences.

God told the prophet Hosea to marry Gomer the prostitute to illustrate how he felt about the wanton disobedience of Israel when they failed to keep the covenant relationship with him. The nation of Israel intermarried with people who worshipped foreign gods, and broke many other laws which their forefathers had covenanted to keep when Moses first presented the Ten Commandments to them at Sinai. Despite rescuing her from a fallen lifestyle, Hosea's kindness was repaid with betrayal when Gomer returned to her old ways.

What promises have we made to God? Have we kept them or are we prostituting our faith?

God's promises are irrevocable – he is trustworthy. 'God is not a man, that he should lie, nor a son of man, that he should change his mind. Does he speak and then not act? Does he promise and not fulfil?' (Numbers 23:19).

THEMES

Covenant
Marriage
Promises

BIBLE REFERENCES

Genesis 22:15–18
Joshua 21:45; 23:14–15
1 Kings 8:56
Psalms 110:4; 145:13
Isaiah 45:23; 55:11
Amos 6:8; 8:7
Malachi 3:6–7
Matthew 5:17

Luke 4:16–21; 24:49
John 3:34–35
Acts 1:4; 2:29–31
Romans 4:21
2 Corinthians 1:18–20
Galatians 3:22
Ephesians 1:13–14
Titus 1:2
2 Timothy 1:1
Hebrews 6:13–18; 8:6–8; 10:23
James 1:17–18
2 Peter 1:3–4

54 Overcome by Anger ✓ 4/07 6.70

French newspapers reported that when Christine Hupier was refused a loan by her bank manager, she was so angry that she took off her clothes, applied superglue to her body and then stuck herself to the astonished official. Police charged her with damaging the bank manager's expensive Armani suit.

Anger also overcame a technician at a Canadian aircraft factory. Having been told he was sacked, he refused to go quietly. Instead the Scottish worker put on a kilt, hoisted himself up on a crane and brought the factory to a complete standstill for three hours by playing the bagpipes.

APPLICATION

Think back to the last time you felt anger and rage over something. How was that anger expressed? It is not always wrong to be angry. Sometimes anger is an appropriate reaction to the way we or other people have been treated. However, the way our anger is expressed is the defining moment.

Two brothers killed the population of a whole town when one of its inhabitants raped their sister (Genesis 34). Their anger was justified, but their actions were wrong and sinful (Genesis 49:5–7). Some people lose their temper when they get angry, and become violent or use offensive or threatening words and behaviour. Others boil up inside and get stressed and unhappy but try not to let it show.

God's anger by comparison is never personal or petty. What makes God angry is taking advantage of the orphan or widow (Exodus 22:22–24), or breaking a serious promise or covenant (Deuteronomy 29:22–28). Also, God balances his anger with love – he is the perfect judge. The Bible says time and again that God is slow to get angry, and that we should leave vengeance to God.

THEMES

Anger
Temper

BIBLE REFERENCES

Exodus 4:14; 11:8; 16:20; 22:22–24; 32:10, 19; 34:6
Numbers 11:1, 10; 16:15; 22:22
Deuteronomy 7:4; 9:19; 11:16–17; 29:27; 31:17
1 Samuel 11:6; 20:34
Psalms 2:12; 30:5; 37:8; 56:7; 74:1; 79:5; 80:4; 85:5; 86:15; 102:9–10; 103:8; 145:8
Proverbs 19:3; 29:22
Ecclesiastes 7:9
Lamentations 3:22
Hosea 5:10; 11:9
Matthew 5:22
Mark 3:5; 10:14
Luke 14:21
Romans 5:9
1 Corinthians 13:5
Galatians 5:19–20
Ephesians 4:26, 31; 6:4
Colossians 3:8, 21
1 Timothy 2:8
Titus 1:7
James 1:19–20
Revelation 6:16

55 Pain for One Pound

A game of pain is gaining a cult following at London's Segaworld. Instead of the usual electronic arcade games, this £1-a-try thriller involves pain not pleasure. The volunteer (or is it victim?) sits in a chair which simulates the electric chair used to execute convicted killers in some US states. 'The Shocker' tests your endurance by increasing its 'voltage', which is actually high speed vibrations sent into your body through rubber levers which you grip. The longer you keep hold, the higher the volts/vibrations. Hit 2,000 volts and it starts smoking.

Crowds of youngsters – keen to show their mates how tough they are – can be seen trying out 'The Shocker' most days.

APPLICATION

According to the Bible, God takes pleasure in his people (Psalm 149:4) and no pleasure at all in the death of the wicked (Ezekiel 18:23).

THEMES

Pain
Pleasure

BIBLE REFERENCES

Job 33:19
Psalm 149:4–5
Ecclesiastes 7:3
Ezekiel 18:23, 32; 33:11
Ephesians 5:8–10
1 Thessalonians 4:1
2 Timothy 2:3; 4:5

56   Pay as You Go

When a man arrived at the Accident and Emergency Department of a Brazilian hospital, the staff were amazed to find a mobile phone jammed up his bottom! The patient told doctors that he had slipped in the shower and landed on his mobile phone which he had left on the bathroom floor. The situation turned into a farce when, during the prolonged efforts of the doctor to remove the phone, it rang three times.

'We wondered if he had an answering machine up there as well,' said one of the doctors to Rio newspaper reporters afterwards.

In another strange but true adventure from Brazil, a fishing expedition turned nasty when an angler got his line caught up in a bees' nest. He was then chased by the angry insects along the banks of the Amazon. Desperate to escape the stinging bees, the man jumped into the water and was eaten alive by deadly piranhas!

APPLICATION

What is the most stupid thing you've ever done?

An unwise decision or action can suddenly result in a highly dangerous situation. That extra drink for the road before climbing behind the wheel of a car, that apparently innocent flirting with a married man/woman, and a host of other situations can develop from an unwise choice into a tricky, embarrassing or even life-threatening dilemma.

Wisdom and discernment are gifts of the Holy Spirit. James 1:5 recommends that anyone who realises they lack wisdom should ask for help from God, who can give us the extra knowledge that we lack.

The writer of Ecclesiastes (most scholars believe it was Solomon) was considered the wisest man ever to have lived. 'Wisdom is better than strength,' he writes in Ecclesiastes 9:16. Proverbs 16:16 records that it is 'better to get wisdom than gold'.

THEMES

Foolishness
Wisdom

BIBLE REFERENCES

Deuteronomy 4:6
1 Samuel 25:25
1 Kings 3:9, 28; 4:29–31; 5:12; 10:4–7
2 Chronicles 1:10; 9:3–6
Job 12:12–16; 32:7
Psalms 14:1; 90:12; 104:24; 111:10; 119:98
Proverbs 3:19; 4:5–7; 9:6; 10:1; 15:20; 16:16; 17:25; 19:13; 21:30; 24:14
Ecclesiastes 2:13; 9:16; 10:1
Isaiah 28:29
Jeremiah 10:14
Daniel 2:20–22; 11:33; 12:3
Hosea 7:11
Matthew 10:16; 12:42; 13:54; 25:2
Mark 7:20–22
Luke 2:40; 11:31; 12:20; 24:25
Acts 6:3
Romans 1:22; 11:33; 16:27

1 Corinthians 1:21–25; 3:19; 12:8
Galatians 3:1
Ephesians 1:8; 3:10
Colossians 2:3
2 Timothy 3:15
James 1:5

57   Phone Pest

Have you ever been annoyed by someone sitting near you on a bus or train who is using a mobile phone? On one occasion a young man was talking loudly on his mobile phone on a commuter train – so loudly that the people sitting next to him got annoyed and moved away. But soon everyone in the train carriage could hear the man talking, and they became increasingly disturbed and frustrated by his noise.

After five minutes of talking and shouting the man ended his conversation. Things were just settling down to normality when a middle-aged man in the carriage clutched his chest and cried out in pain. It was obvious to everyone that he was suffering a heart attack.

Someone suggested that they should pull the emergency cord and stop the train. But they quickly realised that this wouldn't help – they needed to get to the next station and then call for an ambulance.

'I know,' said one lady. 'Let's dial 999 on that man's mobile phone. That way the ambulance can be waiting for us at the next station.'

Everyone agreed that this was a good idea.

'Quick, phone for an ambulance,' the woman told the young man with the mobile phone.

With everyone looking at him expectantly the man blushed bright red and had to admit that the phone he had been using earlier was a toy and not a real mobile phone at all!

A certain night club in Liverpool is built in a basement. It has a thick concrete ceiling which makes mobile phones useless. Nevertheless, each week the bar staff notice young men using mobile phones in an attempt to impress their girlfriends. The staff know for certain that the lads are posing but hide their amusement to spare the feelings of the young men!

APPLICATION

What props do you use to convey an image or give an impression that isn't accurate or true? God is not fooled by outward appearance – he sees our hearts (1 Samuel 16:7; Matthew 23:27). If we pretend to be something or someone that we are not, we will eventually be found out (Numbers 32:23).

THEMES

Appearance
Deception
Embarrassment
Masks
Pretence
Reality

BIBLE REFERENCES

Numbers 32:23
1 Samuel 16:7
Matthew 23:27–28

58 Plain Speaking

Political correctness is flourishing in the USA. One official document described a car crash victim as being in a 'non-viable condition' (he was dead). Other similar government jargon details how an aeroplane 'suffered an involuntary conversion' (it crashed), while a dead hospital patient was described as 'the victim of a negative patient care outcome'.

It seems this creeping disease is invading Britain also. For instance, Surrey County Council has outlawed the familiar rural sign 'Beware of the bull' because it said the words were 'too scary'. Local farmers have been given replacement notices which warn: 'Proceed with caution. Bull in field.' The senior rights-of-way officer told the *Daily Mail*: 'It is illegal to put up a sign that deters or gives the wrong impression. We feel the old wording is just the wrong side of the line.'

Meanwhile in Bristol a woman is seeking compensation from her local supermarket because she feels they are deliberately positioning the bananas in fruit racks in a suggestive and provocative way!

APPLICATION

In some cases political correctness goes too far and becomes ridiculous. Describing a dead person as being in a 'non-viable condition' is dressing up a harsh but true fact and seeking to make it less shocking and more palatable.

Some things are and should remain shocking. A lack of frank and open talking in a misguided attempt to protect a person may do more harm than good. Death, for example, has become a taboo subject among some people, but one out of every one person dies. It is something we need to be honest and open about!

Similarly, hell is a rarely preached topic in most churches. It is almost as though we are ashamed that God could send a person to hell. But Jesus spoke more about hell than heaven – presumably because he didn't want anyone apart from Satan and his demons to go there. While not going over the top about these subjects, death, hell and other topics must be addressed openly and honestly as we study the Bible.

THEMES

Death
Hell
Honesty
Political correctness

BIBLE REFERENCES

Job 15:2
Psalm 89:48
Proverbs 17:27; 20:15; 25:11
Ecclesiastes 7:2; 10:13–14
Matthew 5:29–30; 10:28; 13:42, 50; 18:8–9; 23:33
Mark 8:32; 9:43–48
Luke 12:5
John 7:13; 10:24; 11:14; 16:25, 29; 18:20
2 Corinthians 3:12
Hebrews 9:27

59   Poor Spend More at Christmas

Struggling families spend more on Christmas presents for their children than wealthy parents, according to a survey in a women's magazine. Couples earning less than £12,000 a year are likely to spend more on a gift than higher-paid families, because of pride and pressure from TV advertising.

Low earners often plunge themselves into debt with a festive spending spree just so their children will not feel left out, claims the survey. Welfare groups say poorer families find it impossible to refuse when their children ask for expensive toys advertised on television.

A spokesperson for the one-parent organisation Gingerbread said, 'I think all parents would breathe a sigh of relief if ads aimed at children were banned from the small screen.'

The survey revealed that 70 per cent of mothers believed gift choices were dictated by TV adverts.

APPLICATION

How much does the media (TV, radio, magazines and adverts on hoardings, etc) affect you or your family's aspirations about Christmas presents?

Should adverts for toys be banned to prevent parents from being pressurised? Do you think children/teenagers expect more, the same or less than they did fifteen years ago?

What do you think is God's attitude towards possessions?

THEMES

Advertising
Christmas
Media

BIBLE REFERENCES

Proverbs 30:8–9
Isaiah 55:2
Matthew 13:22
Luke 12:15

60   Pre-Teen Beauty Queen

Aged just eleven, Blaire Ashley Pancake (her real name) had already won over ninety beauty contests. Blaire, from Chattanooga, Tennessee, has been taking part in beauty pageants since the age of six!

After carefully applying her lipstick, and polish on her false fingernails, she practises her lines. 'If you could be anyone in the world, who would you be?' prompts proud father Bruce, a plastic surgeon.

'Why, I'd be myself,' replies Blaire, with a well-rehearsed smile that almost looks natural.

As well as £8,000 cash, Blaire has won countless hair-dryers, half a dozen TVs and a car. 'Being in beauty contests is the only thing that interests me,' says Blaire. 'They're all I want to do. One day I want to be Miss America.'

APPLICATION

What is your initial reaction to this story? Is there any harm in entering children and young people into beauty contests?

What effect will these contests have on the way Blaire feels about herself? Do people who are 'good-looking' have a big advantage in life? Do you think Blaire's father's occupation is significant?

THEMES

Appearance
Beauty
Obsession

BIBLE REFERENCES

1 Samuel 16:7
Proverbs 31:30
1 Peter 3:3–4

61 Pricey Present

A man went to a toy shop to buy his young daughter a Barbie doll for her birthday. As he browsed along the shelves he spotted 'Barbie Goes Horse Riding', which cost £19.99, and 'Barbie At The Beach' which also cost £19.99. Finally he saw 'Barbie Gets A Divorce' which had a price tag on it of £129.99.

'How come this Barbie is so expensive?' he asked the shop assistant.

'That's because as well as a Barbie doll that set also includes Ken's house, Ken's car, Ken's yacht, Ken's caravan . . .'

APPLICATION

When a marriage fails, there are physical, mental, social and spiritual costs as well as financial costs!

'The only grounds for divorce in California are marriage' (Cher).

'"I hate divorce," says the Lord' (Malachi 2:16).

THEMES

Divorce
Marriage

BIBLE REFERENCES

Deuteronomy 24:1–4
Malachi 2:16
Matthew 1:19; 5:31–32; 19:3–9
Mark 10:2–11
Luke 16:1–8
1 Corinthians 7:11

62 Promises, Promises

Are you good at keeping your promises?

When the Pensioners' Party failed to win any seats in the Czech Republic General Election in 1998, its leader kept a pre-election promise. He had vowed that if they did badly he would eat a live beetle. He duly kept his promise and swallowed a wriggling bug!

APPLICATION

Some promises rashly made are unwise. The beetle-eating may have been distasteful, but some rash promises have far worse consequences. The story of Jephthah is a dramatic example: his promise resulted in the death of his beloved daughter (Judges 11:30–40).

The value of a promise depends on the reliability and trustworthiness of the person who makes the promise. God will never break his promises – they are irrevocable. His covenant relationship with Israel is an example of God keeping his promises, while humans often break their side of the deal.

As God's Son, Jesus has the right to make promises on God's behalf (John 3:34–35; Hebrews 1:1–3).

Promises of God in Christ include:

- Forgiveness of sins (1 John 1:9)

- Resurrection (John 5:29)

- The fullness of life and eternal life (John 10:10; 2 Timothy 1:1)

150

- The gift of the Holy Spirit (Luke 24:49)
- The knowledge of God (1 John 5:20)
- The peace of God (Philippians 4:4–9)

'From the promise to the deed is a day's journey' (Bulgarian proverb).

THEMES

God's trustworthiness
Promises

BIBLE REFERENCES

Genesis 22:15–18
Numbers 23:19; 30:1–2
Joshua 21:45; 23:14–15
1 Kings 8:56
Psalms 50:14; 145:13
Luke 24:49
John 3:34–35; 5:29; 10:10
Romans 4:21
2 Corinthians 1:18–20
Philippians 4:4–9
2 Timothy 1:1
Hebrews 1:1–3; 10:23
1 John 1:9; 5:20

63 Propelling Priests

The staff of a bank in Seville, Spain, couldn't understand why their revolving door was injuring so many members of the clergy. Whenever a priest or nun used the door it suddenly speeded up and threw them out the other side. Over twenty clerics suffered excessive spinning, including two elderly nuns who were rotated thirteen times before being rescued. One priest tried unsuccessfully to exorcise the door.

It took undercover police to discover the cause – a Muslim security guard, who speeded up the door from his control desk whenever he saw a Christian cleric approach.

APPLICATION

Jesus warned his followers that they would face opposition and sometimes persecution for being a disciple of Christ. Today, Christians are facing a variety of opposition worldwide. In some countries they are making the ultimate sacrifice for their faith and conscience, while in most Western countries the opposition is more subtle.

Believers who face opposition are instructed by the Bible to endure (1 Corinthians 4:12) and to love and pray for their persecutors (Matthew 5:44; Romans 12:12). Peter reminds his readers not to be surprised by trials 'but rejoice that you participate in the sufferings of Christ, so that you may be overjoyed when his glory is revealed' (1 Peter 4:13).

THEMES

Persecution
Religious intolerance

BIBLE REFERENCES

Matthew 5:10–11, 44; 10:23; 13:21; 23:34
Mark 4:17
Luke 21:12
Acts 7:52
Romans 12:12–14
1 Corinthians 4:12
2 Corinthians 4:8–9
Galatians 6:12
1 Thessalonians 3:4
2 Thessalonians 1:4
2 Timothy 3:12
1 Peter 4:13, 19

64   Putting Milk Before a Monarch!

A milkman who was given the MBE for 'services to the community' surprised his customers by turning down an invitation to Buckingham Palace because he didn't want to disrupt his milk round.

Trevor Jones, aged 69, has been delivering a daily pinta in Tredegar since he was six. Known to locals as 'Jones the Milk', he was nominated for the award by his satisfied customers.

However, Mr Jones told a *Daily Telegraph* reporter that making the trip to London for the ceremony would be too disruptive: 'The Queen is a very nice lady, but she isn't worth rushing for. I'm sure she will understand.'

APPLICATION

Jones the Milk would rather serve his customers than meet the Queen. He preferred to stick with the people he knew and served daily, rather than take the chance to visit an important stranger.

Sometimes when people have the opportunity to be with important or famous people they forget their 'true' friends, often realising only too late that meeting glitzy stars might be fun, but true friendship is something more valuable. If you suddenly inherited a vast fortune, would you continue to mix with your old friends?

The Prodigal Son discovered that his new 'friends' suddenly left him once his money ran out (Luke 14:13–16).

THEMES

Friends
Loyalty

BIBLE REFERENCES

Genesis 2:18
Ruth 1:16–18
1 Samuel 22:14
Proverbs 20:6
Amos 3:3
1 Corinthians 15:33

65 Quids for Questions

A man asked a lawyer how much it would cost to answer just three simple questions. The lawyer replied, '£500.'

'£500? Isn't that pretty expensive?' said the man.

'Not really,' retorted the lawyer, obviously annoyed. 'Now what is your third question?'

APPLICATION

If you could ask any person in the world a question, who would you ask and what would the question be?

The Pharisees and religious leaders asked Jesus many questions. However, most were asked in an attempt to trick Jesus and were not honest attempts to discover truth. What questions would you like to ask God?

THEMES

Questions
Tests

BIBLE REFERENCES

Exodus 12:26
Joshua 4:6, 21
Matthew 16:13; 22:35, 46
Mark 4:10; 7:17; 8:29; 13:3
Luke 2:46; 11:53; 17:20; 23:9
John 18:9
Acts 5:27; 22:24

66   Revenge Is Sweet

Revenge, as they say, is sweet. Now an American best-selling book offers wronged wives and lovers a host of ways to get even with the men who have let them down.

The Woman's Book of Revenge is written by Christine Gallagher, who said: 'The desire for revenge is an inevitable step on the road to recovery. Revenge is not a dirty word, it's a time-honoured tradition. It's a way of bringing the scales of justice back into proper balance.' Her book outlines hundreds of ways of seeking revenge, all said to be drawn from real-life incidents.

One woman called the Australian talking clock from her ex-boyfriend's phone and then left the receiver off the hook for days while he was on holiday. He returned to a £6,000 bill! Gallagher helpfully provides the number to call!

Another woman featured in the book alerted her ex-lover's boss that he had once confided that much of his CV was pure invention. A third sold her ex-husband's Porsche for £30.

Other revenge tactics detailed include cutting the elastic waist band in all his underpants, cutting a small hole in the rear of his swimming trunks, and tearing out a few pages from his favourite books.

Gallagher also suggests putting an Oxo cube in the shower head, placing an open can of sardines in a heating vent or replacing his haemorrhoid cream with Vick's Vapour Rub!

157

APPLICATION

Is revenge so sweet? It might settle our sense of justice, but it rarely heals a wound – more usually inflaming it and extending the period before healing can take place.

The Bible teaches that neither passionate nor premeditated revenge is right. Justice must be done, but this must be left in the hands of God, or the authorities ordained by God. God says, 'It is mine to avenge; I will repay' (Deuteronomy 32:35; Romans 12:19; Hebrews 10:30).

THEMES

Anger
Revenge

BIBLE REFERENCES

Genesis 4:15
Leviticus 19:18
Numbers 31:2; 35:12
Deuteronomy 19:21; 32:35
Joshua 20:3–9
Judges 15:7; 16:28
1 Samuel 25:26–33
2 Samuel 14:11; 22:48
2 Chronicles 24:22
Psalms 9:12; 79:10; 94:1; 149:6–7
Proverbs 20:22
Jeremiah 11:20; 20:12
Ezekiel 25:12–15
Joel 3:21
Nahum 1:2
Matthew 5:38–42
Acts 7:24
1 Peter 3:9
Revelation 6:10

67 Richest Man in the Cemetery

Oprah Winfrey, the famous American television personality, once spent £20 million in just one year. She said, 'I'm blessed with more money than I could ever use – I'm so lucky!'

But lots of money doesn't guarantee happiness or good health. The Bible warns against putting too much trust in money. Jesus once told the story of a farmer who got rich (Luke 12:13–21). He built huge barns to store all his grain and then announced to everyone that he would eat, drink and be merry. But God said the farmer was a fool, because that night he was going to die – and what use would all his riches be to him then?

Colonel Sanders of Kentucky Fried Chicken fame once said: 'There's no reason to be the richest man in the cemetery. You can't do any business there.'

Having lots of money is not in itself wrong, but the love of money is. The Bible describes the love of money as the root of all kinds of evil (1 Timothy 6:10). God wants us to be spiritually rich and to store up treasures in heaven, not on earth.

APPLICATION

How much money is enough? How much money does a person need to be regarded as rich in the UK? What about in a poor, underdeveloped country?

If you didn't have to worry about having enough money, how would your life change? Do you have a balanced attitude towards money? If you suddenly inherited a lot of money, how would it affect and change you? How would it affect your relationships with others?

'Money is a singular thing. It ranks with love as man's greatest source of joy. And with death as his greatest source of anxiety' (J. K. Galbraith, *The Economist*).

THEMES

Death
Money

BIBLE REFERENCES

Job 22:24
Psalms 19:9–10; 119:127
Proverbs 8:19; 16:16; 19:10
Ecclesiastes 5:10
Zephaniah 1:18
Matthew 6:19–21; 13:22
Luke 6:24; 16:13
1 Timothy 6:6–10
2 Timothy 3:2–5
Hebrews 13:5
James 2:2–5

68   Right Place, Right Time

Have you ever had the experience of being in exactly the right place at the right time? It happened to a man who had a heart attack halfway through a plane journey.

When Klaus Schmidt, sixty-four, crashed onto the floor, the airline steward asked, 'Is there a doctor on board?' and forty hands shot in the air! These belonged to a delegation of German heart specialists who were returning home from a medical conference in Ireland. Needless to say the man's life was saved!

APPLICATION

The story of how Philip is told by the Holy Spirit to go and stand by a road in the desert is a classic example of a divine appointment (Acts 8:26–40). God knew that an official from the Ethiopian court would be travelling on the road, searching for spiritual truth. By responding to God's call and guidance, Philip met the man and was able to answer his questions then lead him into faith in Christ. The man was baptised and went on his way rejoicing.

Have you any examples of divine appointments or other aspects of God's guidance? When does a coincidence stop becoming a coincidence?

THEMES

Divine appointment
Guidance

BIBLE REFERENCES

1 Kings 18:12
Isaiah 59:21; 63:11–14
Luke 4:1
John 16:13
Acts 10:37–38; 16:6–7
Romans 8:14, 26–27
1 Corinthians 12:7–11
Galatians 5:18, 25

6.30 mm 07

69   Roaring Drunk

After a long night of drinking beer and spirits, two Indian men decided to visit the local zoo. However, when Prakesh Tiwari, very much the worse for wear, decided to give the tigers some flowers – and crossed a moat to hand them over – he paid for his drunken folly with his life.

Having made a garland of marigolds, he and a friend, Suresh Rai, approached a Royal Bengal tiger. Rai threw the flowers around the animal's neck and it attacked him. When Tiwari kicked the tiger, it turned on him and inflicted fatal wounds.

APPLICATION

Alcohol affects a person's judgement. Reaction times slow, which is why drinking and driving is so dangerous. It also means that people do or say things which they would not dream of doing when sober. Alcohol can lead to folly, reck-lessness, brawling and sometimes death.

THEMES

Alcohol
Drinking and driving

BIBLE REFERENCES

Genesis 9:21; 19:32–35
Psalm 107:27

Proverbs 20:1
Isaiah 5:11, 22
Habakkuk 2:5, 15
Romans 13:13
1 Corinthians 5:11; 6:9–10
Galatians 5:19–21
Ephesians 5:18

70   Saints and Sinners

A vicar was leaving the church building when he was grabbed roughly by the arms and addressed by a local criminal.

'My brother's just died – got stabbed – and I want you to bury him, right? When his coffin is going into the ground, you've got to tell everyone that he was a saint, right? And if you don't tell everyone he was a saint, you'll be joining him – six feet under!'

With that the man turned and left as abruptly as he had arrived.

Five days later, as the coffin was lowered into the grave, the vicar turned to the mourners and spectators and said: 'The deceased was a bully, a villain and cared about no one except himself. He stole, lied, swore, got drunk, sold drugs, was a pimp, blasphemed and was a cruel and violent thug. The local community is glad to see the back of him.

'However, compared to his brother – he was a saint!'

APPLICATION

Most people think of saints as Christians who, when they were alive, were exceptionally holy and pious. However, Paul regularly addressed all Christians as saints. Many of his epistles begin with a salutation 'To all the saints in Ephesus', or wherever it was he was writing to. The fact is that every true believer is a saint.

The Greek word *hagioi*, which we translate as 'saints', literally means 'sanctified' or 'holy ones' – people separated from sin and consecrated to God's sacred service. The saint-hood that you and I enjoy is not an attainment that we have earned, but a state into which God in his grace has called us (2 Timothy 1:9).

Although we are all sinners, if we have experienced Christ's forgiveness and are in fellowship with God, we are saints.

The Bible also consistently calls us to live holy lives (1 Peter 1:14–16; 2 Peter 3:11). Whatever we feel like today – sinners or saints – let's live in the reality that we are called to work hard at being a holy people, offering spiritual sacrifices acceptable to God (1 Peter 2:5).

THEMES

Holiness
Honesty
Saints
Sin

BIBLE REFERENCES

1 Corinthians 3:17
Ephesians 1:1; 2:21
2 Timothy 1:9
1 Peter 1:14–16; 2:5–9
2 Peter 3:11

71 Santa in the Cells ✓ 2/03 /m·

In 1983 a group of happy children were just leaving Santa's grotto in the toy department of a large department store near London, when several policemen arrived. They strode over to Father Christmas, fastened handcuffs on to him, and frogmarched him out of the shop. Santa attempted a few half-hearted 'Yo Ho Ho's' as the amazed elves, who had helped him hand out presents, watched open-mouthed! The store manager later confirmed that Santa was 'taken to the police station and charged with persistent non-payment of traffic fines'.

Like many things about Christmas, Santa isn't quite what he seems at first. He is in fact a combination of the early church Christian Saint Nicolas and the Victorian creation Jack Frost. There are many aspects of Christmas we might accept but which actually have nothing to do with the first Christmas.

APPLICATION

What aspects of Christmas do you enjoy the most? If you could change one thing about the way you celebrate Christmas what would it be?

At Christmas we give gifts to friends and family. What gift do you think God would like to give you, and what gift do you think God would like from you this year?

To discover the true meaning of Christmas we need to go back to the original story as recorded in Matthew's and Luke's Gospels.

THEMES

Christmas
Reality
Surprise

BIBLE REFERENCES

Matthew 1:18–2:18
Luke 2:1–20

72   Saved by the AA Blonde

When Arthur and Jean Wilson's car broke down on the A3 near Guildford, Arthur called the Automobile Association (AA) on his mobile phone. The AA operator assured him a member of staff would arrive within forty-five minutes to give him roadside assistance.

However, when the AA van drew up, out stepped a 21-year-old blonde woman. Georgina Reynolds was the first ever AA patrol woman in eighty-five years. Mr Wilson was so embarrassed that a woman was helping him fix his car, he asked his wife to walk down the road 100 metres to a roadside seat where she would be out of earshot.

Since her yellow van has been out on the Surrey roads, Ms Reynolds has rescued many stranded male drivers. A fully qualified mechanic, she has also been trained to look after herself: 'I've got a big metal bar and I've been shown just where to strike.'

APPLICATION

A stereotype is an oversimplified mental picture or an attitude held of a type of person. An AA patrol woman or a male nursery nurse seems strange to most people. But stereotypes are not just based on sexual gender. What other stereotypes can you think of?

Often the commonly held stereotype of a Christian is that of someone who is weak and needs an emotional crutch. Think of the Christian or churchgoing characters from TV soaps – often these characters are portrayed as weak, hypo-critical or negative in some other way. Why?

Name some Christians who do not fit the weak Christian stereotype.

The Founder of the faith was not weak – despite the 'meek and mild' image that people often give him.

THEMES

Sexism
Stereotypes

BIBLE REFERENCES

Matthew 5:16
1 Corinthians 11:1
Galatians 3:28
1 Peter 2:21

73   Saved by a Stranger

The quick thinking of a stranger at a bus stop saved the life
of a toddler. As far as Mum Alex Sharp was concerned, her
21-month-old son, Abel, was a bit off-colour and she felt a
bus ride to the shops would do him good. Marie Lord
spotted the signs of the killer disease meningitis, and raced
fifty metres to a phone box where she hauled out the man
using it and dialled 999! By the time an ambulance arrived,
the tot was unconscious. Doctors were just in time to treat
Abel, and his condition changed from critical to stable.

The relieved mum said: 'I am so grateful to Mrs Lord. She
saved my son's life. At first I thought she was being a bit dramatic, but when Abel had to be given oxygen in the ambulance I realised he might die.'

Mrs Lord had picked up tips on spotting meningitis from
watching a TV programme. She remembered that sleepiness
and spots were two of the tell-tale signs of the killer brain
bug. Mrs Lord, thirty-eight, a mother of three, said: 'I'm
sure anyone else would have done the same thing. It's every
parent's worst nightmare.'

APPLICATION

Have you ever helped, or been helped by, a stranger?

We all need to be rescued from the result of sin in our lives.
We are all guilty of breaking God's laws, and the punishment
for this is death. But Christ can rescue us, if we choose to call
out to him.

THEMES

Life-saver
Rescue
Salvation
Saviour

BIBLE REFERENCES

1 Chronicles 16:35
Psalms 27:1; 40:17; 65:5; 68:20; 118:14
Isaiah 12:2; 45:21–22
Jeremiah 39:18
Mark 16:16
Luke 18:26; 19:10
John 3:17; 4:42; 12:47
Romans 10:9
2 Corinthians 6:2
Ephesians 2:5, 8
1 Timothy 1:15; 4:10
Hebrews 5:9
2 Peter 2:9

74 Seriously Good Rush

Veteran New Zealand bungee jumper A. J. Hackett set a new record when he jumped from the 590-foot-high observation circle from near the top of the Sky Tower in Auckland in 1998. Two guide ropes were attached to his bungee rope to stop him bouncing into the side of the building.

After performing the jump live on New Zealand television, and having brought traffic to a halt around the tower, Mr Hackett described the jump as 'a seriously good rush'.

Another bungee thrill-seeker was less fortunate: Eric Barcia from Virginia, who was found dead after bungee jumping off a 70-foot-high railway bridge. Barcia used a series of bungee cords tied together, but made a mistake in his calculations. A police spokesman explained: 'The length of the cord he had assembled was greater than the distance between the bridge and the ground!'

APPLICATION

What has been the most exciting and thrilling moment of your life so far? Often, to experience a great thrill, we need to be in a state of fear and tension. Why? Why do you think some people seem to need or seek out thrills, excitement and 'a good rush' more than others?

Matthew records that the whole city of Jerusalem was excited by the arrival of Jesus (Matthew 21:10).

THEMES

Excitement
Mistakes
Risk-taking

BIBLE REFERENCES

Psalm 4:7
Ecclesiastes 3:22
Matthew 18:13; 21:10
Luke 15:5, 9–10, 24, 32
John 2:17

75   Shock Decision

The following two stories illustrate the maxim that the decisions of the legal professions are not always predictable.

Janet Dean from Perth, Australia, was stopped by store detectives and accused of shoplifting. When the police arrived she stripped naked in front of them to prove she had nothing to hide. They promptly arrested her and charged her with indecent exposure.

In another surprise development, burglar Frank Gort broke down and sobbed when he was sentenced by an American judge to seven years in jail. The weeping thief claimed seven was his unlucky number. The understanding judge in San Antonio, Texas, gave him eight years instead!

APPLICATION

According to God's law every human being deserves to die, because we have all sinned and fallen short of his perfect standard. However, in his mercy God sent his Son Jesus to die in our place, taking our punishment upon himself. We can choose to accept his free gift of forgiveness or reject it. Nothing we have or can do will ever mean we deserve God's forgiveness – it is a gift of grace. According to the law we deserve to die, but because of God's great love for us we can escape hell and enjoy a fulfilled life now and eternal life in the future.

THEMES

Gospel
Grace
Justification
Law

BIBLE REFERENCES

John 1:14–17
Romans 3:23–24; 4:25; 5:1, 16–21; 6:14; 8:30; 11:5–6, 22
1 Corinthians 6:11; 15:10
2 Corinthians 1:2; 8:9; 12:9; 13:14
Galatians 2:16
Ephesians 1:6; 2:4–8; 6:24
Philippians 1:2
Colossians 1:2
1 Thessalonians 1:1
2 Thessalonians 1:2
1 Timothy 1:14
2 Timothy 1:9; 4:22
Titus 1:4; 3:7, 15
Philemon 3
Hebrews 12:15; 13:25
1 Peter 1:2; 4:10; 5:12
2 Peter 1:2
Revelation 22:21

76 Spying on Your Teens!

Julie Green, a 55-year-old mother of teenagers, made secret tape recordings of her son's telephone calls to find out whether he was taking drugs. She is one of a growing number of parents in the United States and Europe who are resorting to Cold War espionage techniques to fight drug and alcohol abuse. Bugging their children's phones, installing secret cameras in clock radios, and sending strands of hair retrieved from pillows for analysis at drug laboratories are all part of their desperate measures to prevent their offspring going off the rails.

'I felt absolutely filthy,' Mrs Green told a newspaper after taping her son's calls. 'The last thing I wanted to do was to turn into the KGB in our own house.'

American radio shops sell home surveillance equipment cheaply. Telephone bugs cost $20, while a chemical analysis kit on the Internet costs less than $50 if you want proof from the hair in your teenager's comb, for example, that he or she is taking drugs. Aerosol sprays and chemical-soaked cotton wipes, as simple as home pregnancy kits, can be bought to detect if there is cannabis or other drugs on car seats or other surfaces.

One security company in the United States gets regular requests from parents to bring its dogs to nose around teenage children's bedrooms for hidden supplies of drugs.

Sometimes parents' sleuthing attempts get discovered. One parent who got caught bugging their son's room said, 'All hell broke loose.' Other parents give up spying because they say they cannot bear the feelings of guilt.

Most teens in America and the UK have televisions in their rooms, and growing numbers have telephones and computers with Internet access. Parents increasingly believe they should be able to get to their children, even surreptitiously, because the rest of the world does! But does that excuse their behaviour? Source: *Daily Telegraph*

APPLICATION

If you accidentally came across your child's diary, which is normally kept hidden away, would you read it?

Parental spies run the risk, if caught, of destroying any trust in their relationship with their children. What other actions can parents/children do which will destroy trust? Is the risk of discovery worth it if your teenage child is in danger, and you may be able to take some action to remove them from harm?

What can we do to help build trusting, open relationships where parents and children communicate about their problems and concerns?

THEMES

Drugs
Parents
Trust

BIBLE REFERENCES

Exodus 20:12
Leviticus 19:3
Deuteronomy 5:16
Psalms 27:10; 127:3; 144:12
Proverbs 3:12; 30:17
Malachi 4:6

Matthew 15:4; 19:19
Mark 7:10; 10:19
Luke 14:26; 18:20
Romans 1:30
Ephesians 6:1–4
Colossians 3:20
Hebrews 12:9–11

77 Stupid Is as Stupid Does

55-M mm/03 .

When Laura MacKenzie drew up in her car at a red traffic light on a road in the Australian outback she was in for a long delay. The traffic light remained stuck on red, but she waited patiently for it to change for two whole days!

Eventually another driver found her slumped in the car, suffering from dehydration. 'How was I supposed to know the lights were broken?' said MacKenzie later. 'It was red so I waited for it to change!'

Another example of poor judgement was demonstrated by a New York lawyer. In an effort to win an argument about who held the 100 metres Olympic record, he decided to stage a reconstruction in his office corridor. Unfortunately he misjudged his run and crashed straight out of the window, falling thirty-nine floors to his death.

APPLICATION

Sometimes people do the most stupid things. Imagine waiting for a red light to change for two days, or running through the window of a high-rise building! What examples of stupidity have you witnessed recently? What is the most stupid thing a person could do?

Proverbs 14:7 warns us: 'Stay away from a foolish person.' The company of fools can be dangerous, both to our physical and spiritual well-being.

THEMES

Foolishness
Poor judgement

BIBLE REFERENCES

1 Samuel 13:13
Psalms 14:1; 53:1; 74:22
Proverbs 1:7; 10:1; 19:13; 26:1–12
Ecclesiastes 10:1
Matthew 7:24; 25:2
Luke 12:20
Romans 1:22
1 Corinthians 1:18, 25

78   Surprising Services

It's amazing what some people leave behind in church. In a survey of 400 churches, vicars and ministers were asked to list items of lost property left behind after a church service. As well as the usual collection of umbrellas and Bibles, it was discovered that hearing aids, a baby's dummy, a Filofax, wellies and even a lottery ticket were left in the pews. At one church in south London a vicar found a wheelchair at the end of a Sunday service. The vicar said, 'It was a few weeks before we knew whether or not to claim a miracle.'

Amazingly, the top of the pops for lost property was false teeth! Apparently some older people like to take their dentures out when they sing hymns, but a case of forgetfulness results in the false teeth being left behind.

The survey also revealed that some surprising things happen during church services. For example, at a meeting in a Baptist church, the minister looked up to see two policemen running down the aisle in hot pursuit of a suspect.

And an Anglican vicar was horrified to discover a new use for his surplice when a child in his congregation came forward during a service and was sick in it!

APPLICATION

Forgetfulness is sometimes seen as part of getting old. However, the Bible warns against forgetting God's ways, words and past blessings.

What has been the most surprising thing that you have seen happen in a church service? When the disciples met together to pray after Jesus' ascension to heaven, they were surprised when God's Holy Spirit descended in power into the room. They heard the sound of a wind, and flames of fire appeared above their heads. Then they went outside and talked with many people of various nationalities in their own languages, causing more surprise and amazement (Acts 2).

THEMES

Forgetfulness
Surprise

BIBLE REFERENCES

Deuteronomy 6:12; 8:11
Judges 8:33–34
Nehemiah 9:17
Psalms 50:22; 78:42

79 Tales of the Unexpected

A man was sitting in a bar enjoying a drink after work, when an exceptionally beautiful woman entered. She noticed him appreciating her good looks and walked up to him. Bold as brass she said to him, 'I'll do anything for you, absolutely anything, for £100, on one condition. You have to tell me what you want me to do in just three words.'

The man considered the proposition for a moment, withdrew his wallet from his pocket and slowly counted out five twenty-pound notes, which he pressed into her hand. He looked deep into her eyes and said, 'Paint my house.'

APPLICATION

When Jesus asked the Samaritan woman for a drink, her first reaction must have been complete surprise. Why was he, a Jewish man, asking her, a Samaritan woman, for a drink? It wasn't normal – the Jews and Samaritans didn't mix and men regarded women as second-class citizens. It was only later that she realised her mistake, for this was no ordinary man, but the Christ (John 4:4–30).

Jesus frequently amazed, surprised and confounded his supporters and critics alike. What other incidents from the Gospels can you think of where Jesus said or did the unexpected?

THEMES

Surprise
Unexpected

BIBLE REFERENCES

Matthew 22:22; 26:8
Mark 10:24
Luke 11:38
John 3:7; 4:4–30

80   Temper, Temper!

Six German psychologists were arrested when a heated debate turned into a violent brawl at a conference in Hamburg – on road rage!

Meanwhile, one Israeli policeman was sent by his bosses to a hypnotist to try to curb his violent temper. The man, one of Tel Aviv's toughest cops, was so affected by the treatment that he let a suspected mass-murderer off with a caution and lent a drunk-driver his car to get home! Although they were glad to see the back of his old temper, the cop's superiors were not enamoured with his new character either, so they fired him.

APPLICATION

Violent images are everywhere. TV and films feature men and women using violence to get their way. Many screen heroes are violent. Many people believe they have been desensitised and are less aware or shocked by violence on screen. There is an ongoing debate about whether or not screen violence leads to real-life acts of violence.

In real life, over one in four married women will be physically assaulted by their husbands. The number of violent crimes seems to be rising year by year.

The Bible is clear: Jesus Christ was not violent (1 Peter 2:23), and God hates violence (Psalm 11:5). Why do you think that is?

THEMES

Temper
Violence

BIBLE REFERENCES

Genesis 6:11–13; 14:14
2 Samuel 22:3
1 Chronicles 22:8–9
Psalms 11:5; 37:8; 55:9; 139:19
Proverbs 14:17; 19:11; 22:24–25
Ecclesiastes 7:8–9
Isaiah 42:1–3; 53:9
Jeremiah 22:3
Ezekiel 45:9
Malachi 2:16
Matthew 2:13; 5:22
Luke 10:30; 22:50–51
Galatians 5:16–21
Ephesians 4:2, 26–31
Philippians 4:5–8
1 Timothy 3:2–3
2 Timothy 1:7; 2:24
Titus 1:7
James 1:19–20
1 Peter 1:13; 2:23

mc 5/03 r.

81 Tenners from Heaven

A sudden shower caught Dennis Hayward by surprise as he drove to work, when it rained £10 notes on his car!

The cascade of money descended as Mr Hayward was driving through a village near Cheltenham, Gloucestershire. The shocked but honest sales and marketing manager stopped and picked up as many of the notes as he could before driving to a local police station to hand the money over. He later discovered the windfall belonged to a pub landlord who had left a money bag containing £2,500 on his car roof as he set off to deposit the cash at his bank. The bag flew into the road and was then hit by Mr Hayward's car, sending hundreds of notes into the air.

Mr Hayward told newspaper reporters: 'It really was like they were falling from the heavens. I picked up as many notes as possible, but split my trousers in the process.'

Michael Gaunt, who ran the pub, got all but £100 of his money back. He gave Mr Hayward a complimentary meal as a reward and paid for him to get a new pair of trousers. Source: *Daily Mail*

APPLICATION

What would you have done – kept the money or handed it in?

Imagine the emotions Mr Gaunt went through when he realised he had lost £2,500 and then heard that all but £100 had been recovered. Have you ever experienced similar feelings of loss and relief? In your opinion was Mr Hayward's reward mean, appropriate or generous?

'Honesty is the best policy.' Discuss this famous saying. Is it true?

THEMES

Honesty
Lost and found
Money
Reward

BIBLE REFERENCES

Leviticus 19:36
Deuteronomy 25:15
2 Kings 12:15
Job 31:6
Proverbs 12:17
Jeremiah 17:10
Matthew 5:12
Luke 15:4–5
2 Corinthians 8:21; 13:7
Ephesians 6:7–8
Philippians 4:8
Hebrews 11:26; 13:18
Revelation 22:12

82   The End?

The headline on the front cover of the *Daily Express* news-paper on 22 April 1998 was: 'The End'. Next to it was a photograph of Linda McCartney riding her favourite horse and the news that the 56-year-old had died of cancer. Her husband, Paul's, last words to her were also revealed: 'You're riding on your beautiful Appaloosa stallion. It's a fine spring day. We're riding in the woods. The bluebells are all out and the sky is clear blue.'

Some people claim that whereas 'sex' was a taboo subject a hundred years ago, today 'death' is taboo. In 1998 the BBC screened the last dying moments of a man in its acclaimed *Human Body* programme. The broadcast attracted enor-mous attention.

The fact is that many people have not seen a dead body. In Western society we are often shielded from death, and yet one out of one person dies! Surely no other subject, which affects everyone, is so little discussed.

APPLICATION

What do you think happens at 'the end'? Do you believe there is an afterlife? Why do many people prefer not to think or talk about death? Why do more people believe in the exis-tence of heaven than in the existence of hell?

The Bible teaches that we have only one life (as opposed to reincarnation) and then face judgement (Hebrews 9:27). How does that make you feel? If you were to die tomorrow, would there be anything you have not done which you would regret not having had time to do?

Mark Twain once said: 'Why is it that we rejoice at a birth and grieve at a funeral? It is because we are not the person involved.' Paul writes: 'Where, O death, is your victory? Where, O death, is your sting?' (1 Corinthians 15:55). What does he mean?

THEMES

Death
End of the world
Funerals
Future
Hope
Remembrance

BIBLE REFERENCES

Psalm 89:48
Ecclesiastes 7:2
John 5:24
Romans 5:12, 14; 6:23; 15:21
1 Corinthians 15:26, 50–57
Hebrews 2:14
Revelation 1:18; 20:14; 21:4

83　The Big Break

Redd Pepper is 'Trailer Man' according to Tom Cox, who writes for the *Guardian*. Apparently, Redd's cinema voice-overs 'make the mind-numbing sound miraculous'. Redd knew there was something amazing about his voice ever since it broke when he was coming down the stairs, aged thirteen. 'It was like "Hi! [squeak] MOMMM [vibrate]",' he recalled.

However, for eighteen years Redd was a train driver on the London underground. To distract himself from the boredom he often played tricks on the passengers.

'One Halloween night I stopped the train, turned the lights out and said: "THIS IS YOUR DRIVER SPEAK-ING . . . OR IS IT? HAA . . . HAA . . . HAAA!" I could hear the screams echoing from the carriages.'

Redd's big break happened one day when the vice president of the Sci-Fi Channel heard him announce a delay on the Bakerloo line and rushed down the platform to ask for his phone number. The very next day, Redd auditioned for the trailer of the blockbuster film *Waterworld*.

Redd recalls: 'As soon as I'd started saying, "In a world where water is all that exists . . .", all these executives were pointing at me, shouting "He's the one!"'

APPLICATION

Have you got a hidden gift or ability that most people don't know about? Redd's gift was revealed when someone heard his station announcement. What situation would reveal your hidden talent to a wider audience?

Some Christians believe that sometimes God arranges for us to meet people or to be in certain places at certain times. Called 'divine appointments', these so-called coincidences often provide a turning point for someone's life. Have you ever had such an occasion, or do you know of someone else's story about a divine appointment? Acts 8:26–39 tells the story of a divine appointment. God told Philip to travel to a desert road where he met a man from Ethiopia who wanted to understand the Bible better. The man became a Christian and was baptised on the spot!

THEMES

Divine appointments
Opportunity
Stewardship

BIBLE REFERENCES

Matthew 25:14–30
Luke 11:9; 19:13–27
John 3:27

84   The Final Fib

Two university students were nearing the end of a three-year degree course. They had achieved good grades in earlier exams and assignments, so they fully expected to collect a first class degree. In fact, the two friends were so confident that as the last weekend for revision before their finals approached, they decided to relax and go to a friend's house for a party on the Saturday night – 200 miles away.

They had a great time, but ate and drank too much. As a result they slept for most of the following day. Feeling the worse for wear, they eventually made it back to campus early on Monday morning. Still feeling tired and hung over, they decided not to try to take the exam then. Waiting until it had finished, they approached the professor in charge of their course to explain why they had missed the crucial finals exam. They explained that they had visited friends on the Saturday, intending to travel home and study, but that they had a flat tyre on the way back and didn't have a spare in the boot. The lengthy delay meant they were late.

The professor listened with a thoughtful expression on his face and then agreed that they could take the exam a day late. The two students were relieved their lie had worked. That night they studied hard and arrived the next day in good time to take the vital test.

The professor placed them in separate rooms and handed each the test questions. The first question, worth five points, was fairly straightforward and on a topic they had both revised well. Then their eyes fell on question two, which said: 'For 95 points, which tyre?'

APPLICATION

Think back to an incident where a lie which you thought had been successful eventually got discovered. Try to remember how you felt when you initially lied, and how you felt when you got caught out.

Why do people lie? Jesus described Satan as 'the father of lies' (John 8:44). The devil's first lie was to Eve when he told her she would not die as a consequence of eating the forbidden fruit in Eden (Genesis 3:4). One chapter later, Cain lied when claiming he did not know where his brother was (Genesis 4:9). Right from the beginning lies and deception have dogged human beings.

THEMES

Exams
Honesty
Lies

BIBLE REFERENCES

Genesis 3:4; 4:9
Leviticus 19:11
Psalm 63:11
Proverbs 12:19, 22; 21:6
Jeremiah 9:5; 23:14
John 8:44
Acts 5:4
Romans 1:25
Ephesians 4:25
Colossians 3:9
Titus 1:2
Hebrews 6:18
Revelation 14:5

85   The Mysterious Room

An Amish boy and his father were visiting a shopping mall. They were amazed by almost everything they saw, but especially by two shiny, silver walls that could move apart and back together again. The boy asked his dad, 'What is this, Father?'

The man (never having seen a lift) responded, 'Son, I have never seen anything like this in my life. I don't know what it is.'

While the boy and his father were watching wide-eyed, an old lady in a wheelchair rolled up to the moving walls and pressed a button. The walls opened and the lady passed between them into a small room. The walls closed and the boy and his father watched as small circles with numbers lit up above the walls.

They continued to watch as the numbers lit up in the reverse direction. The walls opened up again and a beautiful young woman stepped out. The father, not taking his eyes off the young woman, said quietly to his son, 'Go get your mother.'

APPLICATION

What things mystified you as a child? What things still mystify you? There are still many things about the universe that even the cleverest minds do not understand.

'Do you not know? Have you not heard? The Lord is the everlasting God, the Creator of the ends of the earth. He will not grow tired or weary, and his understanding no-one can fathom' (Isaiah 40:28).

The Bible teaches that believers will be changed from their human bodies into heavenly bodies which will not decay or be subjected to tiredness, sickness or death. This is a great mystery.

Jesus once said to his disciples: 'I tell you the truth, unless you change and become like little children, you will never enter the kingdom of heaven' (Matthew 18:3). What did Jesus mean? To discover the answer read what the disciples asked him immediately beforehand (Matthew 18:1).

In a world of change, God is a constant. He does not change; he is eternal. His character, promises, words and ways do not change.

THEMES

Change
Character of God
Mysteries
Transformation

BIBLE REFERENCES

Job 11:7–9
Psalms 135:13; 145:13
Daniel 2:18–47
1 Corinthians 15:51
Ephesians 3:1–6; 5:32
Colossians 1:26–27
Hebrews 13:8
James 1:17
Revelation 1:8

86 The Original Valentine

Behind the cards, chocolates and flowers traditionally given to loved ones on Valentine's Day is a story that goes back over 1,700 years.

Valentine was, according to tradition, a priest in Rome during the reign of Claudius. At this time the Emperor decreed that no man should marry, because he considered that single men made better soldiers in the Roman army.

Valentine was arrested and jailed for secretly marrying young couples. He was told that he would face the death penalty if he didn't renounce his Christian faith and agree not to marry any more courting couples. Despite this threat Valentine refused to turn away from Christ, and while in prison prayed for the blind daughter of a judge to be healed. As a result of her healing, the judge and his family all became Christians and were martyred along with Valentine in the year AD269.

Shortly before the execution, the saint sent the judge's daughter a farewell message which he signed 'from your Valentine'. From this poignant message comes the tradition of sending Valentine cards.

In AD498 Pope Gelasius named 14th February as St Valentine's Day, and ordered a basilica to be built in his honour near the spot where his remains were found.

APPLICATION

Do you believe in anything enough to die for it?

Jesus' suffering and death on the cross shows God's incredible love for each person. The Bible shows us the source, character and value of love. It teaches that we should love one another, and that the greatest commandment is to love God with all our heart, mind, body and spirit.

THEMES

Love
Marriage
Martyrdom
Saints
Values

BIBLE REFERENCES

Leviticus 19:18
Psalms 6:4; 32:10; 51:1; 107:43
Jeremiah 31:3
Lamentations 3:22
Hosea 2:19; 3:1
Matthew 5:44–45; 22:39
Luke 23:34
John 3:16; 5:42; 13:35; 15:12–13
Romans 5:8; 8:38–39; 15:30
1 Corinthians 13
Galatians 5:22
Ephesians 3:17–19; 5:25
1 Thessalonians 3:12
2 Thessalonians 2:13
Hebrews 12:6
1 Peter 1:8
1 John 2:10; 3:16; 4:7–10, 16, 19
Revelation 1:5

87   They're Greedy

Police arrested thirty-eight people in Bristol after tricking them to stay at home in order to take delivery of a supposed 'free gift'. The free gift turned out to be a van load of detectives!

Officers wrote to the last known addresses of eighty people, including burglary suspects and alleged drug pushers, who had failed to appear at court despite receiving summonses. They were all told that they had won a mystery prize and to stay at home for its delivery! The letter told them the pre-paid item was to be delivered by an electrical goods mail order firm, but didn't specify exactly what their prize would be. This was designed to raise their curiosity.

The suspects were told the date and time the delivery would be made to their house. However, it would only be delivered to the named person, making it essential that they were at the address to sign for the package. The 'lucky' suspects were asked to phone a 'winners' hotline' to confirm that they wanted to collect their prize. The call actually connected them to a police station in Bristol!

The 'sting' worked so well that extra court sittings were laid on. Some people even flagged down the delivery vans in the streets near their homes to get their prizes – only to be confronted by plain-clothes detectives.

Detective Inspector Bruce Ballagher told a *Daily Mail* reporter: 'We appealed to the greedy side of people's natures and I was astonished by the response. The phones started ringing straight away and have been red-hot ever since. We expected a 10 per cent pick-up rate but it was far in excess of that – nearly 75 per cent.' He added that the response of those arrested varied from 'complete shock to acute embarrassment'.

APPLICATION

What do you think about the police tactic? Was it cunning or unfair?

The detective inspector said that their tactic had deliberately appealed to the 'greedy side of people's natures'. What is the greedy side of your nature hungry for? What is the best antidote to greed? Is the greedy side of your nature easily satisfied?

THEMES

Greed
Traps

BIBLE REFERENCES

Psalm 10:3
Proverbs 15:27; 28:6–8, 25; 29:4
Amos 8:4–7
Habakkuk 2:5–7
Romans 1:29; 7:8
1 Corinthians 5:10; 6:9–10
Ephesians 4:19; 5:5
Colossians 3:5

88   Tiddly Pooh

A teddy bears' party for children ended in panic and confusion after a drunken man, dressed as Winnie the Pooh, crashed his microlight into a tree. Alan Wombat of Adelaide, Australia, was supposed to be the highlight of the toddlers' party as he flew overhead dressed as a bear and waving to the children below.

However, due to the effects of alcohol, he started to dive-bomb the children instead, shouting 'Winnie's going to get ya!' at the top of his voice. After a few minutes of this he flew into a tree, breaking both his legs.

'Pooh bear used to be my son's hero,' said one angry mother afterwards. 'But now whenever he's mentioned my boy wets the bed.'

APPLICATION

This story graphically illustrates the fact that alcohol affects a person's judgement and speed of reaction. Alcohol can lead to folly, recklessness, unsafe and inappropriate sexual behaviour, brawling and sometimes death.

What are the main reasons why people drink alcohol? Why do some people enjoy getting drunk?

THEMES

Drunkenness
Fear

BIBLE REFERENCES

Genesis 9:21; 19:32–35
Psalm 107:27
Proverbs 20:1
Isaiah 5:11, 22
Habakkuk 2:5, 15
Romans 13:13
1 Corinthians 5:11; 6:9–10
Galatians 5:19–21
Ephesians 5:18

89   Till Death Us Do Part

In 1999 glamorous actress Cameron Diaz told the media that she had agreed to take her unfaithful boyfriend, fellow-actor Matt Dillon, back – but at a price. She demanded that Dillon put £500,000 in a special bank account to ensure he kept his promise to stay faithful. She told him that if he strayed he could say goodbye to her and the cash, which would be given to charity!

Meanwhile in Newark, Nottinghamshire, a bride was so taken by the DJ playing the records for her guests to dance to at the wedding reception, she went on honeymoon with him instead of her new husband!

APPLICATION

Do you think Cameron Diaz's idea was clever or sad? Do you think you will be able to stay faithful to one person? How do you think you would feel if your wife/husband/partner cheated on you?

The Newark bride's promise to her husband lasted less than twelve hours. How long do you think her relationship with the DJ will last?

THEMES

Betrayal
Divorce
Marriage
Promises

BIBLE REFERENCES

Genesis 1:27; 2:18, 23–24
Exodus 20:14
Proverbs 2:16–17; 5:3, 20; 6:32; 7:14–21
Malachi 2:14
Matthew 19:4–5, 18
Mark 10:7–8
Romans 7:2
1 Corinthians 6:9–10; 7:2; 11:11–12
Ephesians 5:31
Hebrews 13:4

90   Too Nice?

A magazine for boys, launched by a mother-of-three, folded after only ten issues because of low sales.

Christine Cubitt wanted *Boys First* to be an updated version of comics such as *The Eagle* and *Victor*, children's favourites from the 1950s and 60s. With her husband and £20,000 of their own money, she began publishing the magazine after her own sons complained there were no decent magazines for them to read.

The monthly contents included features on cars, science, sports and astronomy. At best the magazine sold just over 5,000 copies, but then dropped to just 3,500 per month – well below the target of 20,000 sales. An attempt to increase sales with free sweets on the cover failed when they melted and became fused to the back page.

Mrs Cubitt told the *Daily Mail*: 'We were losing over £2,000 per month. I don't think we were tacky enough to sell on the news stands. It still had a very educational feel about it. There was a lot of sitting down and reading for the children. People don't want that now.'

Publishing colleague Andy Ginn said: 'Kids would rather buy a packet of fags than buy a magazine.'

APPLICATION

The publishers of *Boys First* claimed that articles on fashion, gossip, lifestyle advice and sex are needed to achieve high sales for a magazine to young people. Is that true?

If something is educational and not about sex does that

mean it will be boring to young people? Give reasons for your answer.

Was Mrs Cubitt too old to understand what boys wanted to read about? Maybe the magazine was too boring, and claiming that kids would rather buy fags than a magazine was just an excuse. After all, some teenage magazines sell tens of thousands of copies.

What magazines do you read, and why? If you could launch a magazine, what would it be like?

THEMES

Error
Failure
Reading
Youth culture

BIBLE REFERENCES

Matthew 5:8
Philippians 4:8
1 Timothy 5:22
James 1:27

91   Trapped by Cupboard

A father who tried to retrieve a toy from behind a kitchen cupboard got stuck and had to be rescued by firemen.

John Gueran, a teacher, was attempting to get his son's walkie-talkie, a Christmas present, when the cupboard toppled on top of him. He was unable to move and became so tightly wedged he found it hard to breathe. Only the prompt actions of his teenage daughter, Christiana, who found a fan to pump air into the cupboard, prevented the 42-year-old man from fainting.

The fire brigade was called to the house, where they discovered Mr Gueran trapped with his bottom sticking in the air.

His wife Helen told a *Daily Telegraph* reporter: 'The fire brigade were very good – they could have burst out laughing, but somehow managed to stop themselves.'

The walkie-talkie remains behind the cupboard.

APPLICATION

The gods of the Canaanites were a snare to the nation of Israel, enticing them to practise paganism (Deuteronomy 7:16). Other gods, the work of Satan and his angels, and searching after money, are all described in the Bible as potential snares which distract us and prevent us from following God.

THEMES

Money
Traps

BIBLE REFERENCES

Exodus 23:33
Deuteronomy 7:16
Judges 2:3; 8:27
2 Samuel 22:6
Psalms 91:3; 106:36; 141:9
Luke 21:34
John 8:6
1 Timothy 3:7; 6:9
2 Timothy 2:25–26

92 Truly Thankful

The tradition of saying grace before a meal is fading fast, and where it does take place it usually consists of: 'For what we are about to receive, may the Lord make us truly thankful.'

Fed up with saying the same old thing, a group of Yorkshire businessmen published a book with over seventy graces. A Methodist minister had the idea after receiving enquiries from nervous businessmen asking for help. From time to time members of the Rotary club would be asked to say grace at a club lunch or other function and got bored with the same grace each time. They contacted the minister for advice, which prompted him to write the book. Some of the graces are listed below:

Give us a heart as big as our belly,
And a keen eye which sees the smaller plate of those in need.

Thank you, Lord, for breakfast, lunch and now this dinner.
Without your kindness we would all be a lot thinner.

Lord bless this food upon these dishes,
As thou dost bless the loaves and fishes.
And like the sugar in the tea,
May all of us be stirred by thee.

For ham and eggs and buttered toast,
Praise Father, Son and Holy Ghost.

APPLICATION

Why is it a good thing to say thank you for our food and other good things?

Some say: 'The only time you appreciate something or someone is when they are missing.' Is this true, and if so why?

Communion provides us with an opportunity to remind ourselves of what Jesus did so that we could know God and be welcomed into his family. It gives us the chance to remember Christ's sacrifice and thank him for dying for us.

THEMES

Communion
Thankfulness

BIBLE REFERENCES

1 Chronicles 16:8
Psalms 7:17; 28:7; 30:12; 95:2; 100:4; 107:1; 136:1
Matthew 26:27
1 Corinthians 11:24
Colossians 2:6–7; 3:15
1 Thessalonians 5:18
Hebrews 12:28

93 Twit Twoo!

An amateur birdwatching enthusiast who had been listening to the call of owls in his back garden became excited when they called back to him as he mimicked them.

Neil Simmons began recording in a notebook each occasion when his imitations met with a hooted response. However, unknown to him, his neighbour Fred Cornes was enjoying the same experience.

Mr Cornes enjoyed taking an evening walk in his garden, and when he heard the owls hooting he would playfully respond. For almost a year the two men hooted at each other in the darkness, until one day their wives discussed their husbands' nocturnal habits – and the penny dropped.

'They stopped laughing only long enough to tell us what had happened,' said Mr Simmons. 'I checked my logs and realised that the hoots I had been recording were in fact from Fred. The trouble is, owl calls are not that precise and it is easy to make a mistake.'

Mr Simmons had thought the calls were from two male tawny owls roosting in an old oak tree at the end of his garden. Mr Cornes said he was flattered that his neighbour, who had studied owls in great detail, had mistaken his calls. 'I never realised I sounded so realistic,' he said.

APPLICATION

When Samuel was still a boy, God spoke to him. At first he didn't recognise God's voice. However, in time Samuel became practised at listening to God, and throughout his life was recognised by people as being a prophet.

Some examples of God's voice:

- God's quiet voice (1 Kings 19:12; Job 26:14)

- God's loud voice (Deuteronomy 5:22; John 12:28–29)

- God's voice is awe-inspiring (Psalm 29:3–9; Hebrews 12:18–19, 26)

- Jesus' voice is recognisable (John 10:1–5; 10:14–16)

- Jesus' voice raises the dead (John 5:25, 28; 11:43)

- Jesus' voice calls people to him (Acts 9:4–7; Revelation 3:20)

Some characteristics which should identify a person as being a Christian:

- Compassionate (Colossians 3:12)

- Content (Philippians 4:4)

- Holy (1 Peter 1:15)

- Humble (1 Peter 5:5)

- Joyful (1 Thessalonians 5:16)

- Loving (1 John 4:7)

- Meek (Matthew 5:5)

- Merciful (Luke 6:36)

- Pure in heart (2 Corinthians 11:2–3)

THEMES

Deception
Discernment
Embarrassment
Foolishness
Identity
Mistakes

BIBLE REFERENCES

Jeremiah 29:8
1 Corinthians 6:9–10; 15:33
Galatians 6:7
Ephesians 5:6
Colossians 2:8; 3:12
2 Thessalonians 2:3
1 John 3:7; 4:7

94 Snappy Swimmers 2/2/03 /.

Local politicians have banned a swimming coach from using a crocodile to encourage his young swimmers to swim faster.

Mark Biggles, who teaches swimmers aged seven to twenty in Darwin, Australia, had planned to use the reptile – drugged and with its jaws wired shut – from a local crocodile park. The impact of a crocodile in a swimming pool can only be imagined, but Mark obviously reckoned it would provide the ultimate incentive to swim more quickly!

'Public swimming pools are for people, not for crocodiles,' said a spokesman for Darwin City Council. 'And we do not condone the stress to a crocodile that must ensue from being put in chlorinated water.'

Never mind the stress to the crocodile – what about the stress to the swimmers?!

APPLICATION

What incentives do you use to help you achieve progress in your life? Some people reward themselves with chocolate or other favourite foods when they complete a task or do something well. Shops also use incentives to attract custom and higher sales. Try to list some of the different incentives they use (e.g. buy two and get one free).

Many occupations have a performance-related salary scheme that rewards hard work or high sales with extra pay or other perks. The fact is most people perform better if they are given incentives of this kind.

What incentives are there to living a godly life? What incentives are there to living to please yourself and ignoring the needs of others? What are the most and least attractive aspects of being a Christian and living according to God's requirements?

What is the most powerful incentive: fear of punishment for doing wrong or the desire to win a prize for doing good?

'Fear is the biggest barrier in anyone's life. Fear destroys human potential. Faith gives courage' (Imran Khan, former test cricket captain for Pakistan).

THEMES

Fear
Heaven
Hell
Motivation

BIBLE REFERENCES

Matthew 5:22–30; 6:20; 10:28; 18:3, 9; 19:4
Mark 9:43–47; 10:21
Luke 12:5; 16:23; 18:22
Romans 10:6
1 Corinthians 9:24
Philippians 3:14, 20
2 Timothy 4:18
1 Peter 1:3–4
2 Peter 2:4

95   Stupid Rules

A man's off-road vehicle broke down in the middle of Death Valley in the American Mojave desert. It was the middle of summer, and knowing the area is not named 'Death Valley' for nothing, he decided to walk to find help. By the time he finally reached even a dirt road, he was on his last legs and dying of thirst. Then up ahead he spotted a roadside shop and stumbled up to the door.

'Water!' he croaked.

Morris, the owner of the shop, smiled. 'Hey, I don't sell water. My brother, Sam, runs a diner a mile down the road – he could sell you water. I sell ties . . . wanna buy a tie?'

'No, I need water,' the dying man said. So he dragged himself for a mile in the blistering heat to the door of Sam's restaurant, hauled himself up on his feet and started to walk in, when Sam stopped him.

'Sorry, you can't get in without a tie!'

APPLICATION

As a child I was told I had to wear a smart shirt and tie to go to church because it showed respect. When I protested my mother said: 'If you went to visit the Queen you'd dress up, but we're going to see the King of kings – so put on your tie!'

What stupid or overly strict rules to do with clothing can you think of? Do you think God takes much notice of the clothes we wear when we go to church? Are there any other stupid rules that some people have about church?

THEMES

Appearance
Church
Law

BIBLE REFERENCES

1 Samuel 16:7
Acts 17:24
Galatians 2:6

96 Surprise, Surprise

When a man attempted to steal petrol from a motor home parked on a street, he got much more than he bargained for.

Police arrived at the scene to find the man curled up next to the motor home, being very sick by a pool of spilled sewage. A police spokesman said that the man admitted to trying to steal petrol by inserting a flexible hose into the tank of the motor home. The trouble was, when he began to siphon off the liquid, he realised his mistake – it wasn't the petrol tank he'd inserted the hose into but the van's sewage tank instead.

The owner of the vehicle declined to press charges, saying it was the best laugh he'd ever had.

APPLICATION

When was the last time you did something wrong and ended up with more than you bargained for? The Bible says, 'Be sure your sins will find you out.' Is that always true?

There was once some famous correspondence in *The Times* on 'What's wrong with the world?'. The most penetrating letter on the subject – and the shortest – was from G. K. Chesterton, who wrote simply: 'Dear Sir, I am.'

The heart of the human problem is the problem of the heart – we are all sinners, and as Jeremiah 17:9 says: 'The heart is deceitful above all things and beyond cure.'

THEMES

Mistakes
Sin
Surprises
Unexpected

BIBLE REFERENCES

Numbers 32:23
Romans 6:23
1 John 1:7

97   Wartime Prayer

Early in June 1940, Britain held a Day of National Thanksgiving to praise God for answered prayer and deliverance. Two weeks earlier, the country had responded to a call to prayer from King George VI. Newspaper photographs of the time show long queues of people unable to get into a packed Westminster Abbey.

In the days following, a heavy storm broke over Flanders, beginning on Tuesday 28th May. The *Daily Telegraph* on 8th June reported that the 'darkness of the storm and the violence of the rain' meant that British troops were able to retreat to Dunkirk 'with scarcely any interruption from any aircraft, for aircraft were unable to operate in such turbulent conditions'.

This unseasonal weather, which grounded the Luftwaffe squadrons, enabled more than 300,000 British soldiers – ten times the forecast number – to be safely ferried home across the English Channel. This was described as 'miraculous' by the press and by the Prime Minister, Winston Churchill, not least because of the 'great calm' which settled on the Channel.

The *Telegraph* reported: 'Those who are accustomed to the Channel testify to the strangeness of this calm; they are deeply impressed by the phenomenon of nature by which it became possible for tiny craft to go back and forth safely.'

The king called for further prayer during the war.

APPLICATION

'If my people, who are called by my name, will humble them-selves and pray and seek my face and turn from their wicked ways, then will I hear from heaven and will forgive their sin and will heal their land' (2 Chronicles 7:14).

Jesus promised that he would be present in special power whenever two or three of his disciples met for prayer (Matthew 18:19–20).

'The glorious fact about prayer is that we do not have to pretend with God. He knows all about us anyway. He simply wants us to share every part of our lives with him, and that includes our fears and failings, our moods and emotions, our thoughts and anxieties – everything, even those of which we are deeply ashamed' (David Watson).

THEMES

Prayer
War

BIBLE REFERENCES

Exodus 2:23; 15:1–18
Numbers 20:15–16
Judges 1:1–2; 6:36–40
1 Samuel 12:8
2 Samuel 22:2–51
2 Kings 19:9–11
1 Chronicles 14:11; 16:28–29
2 Chronicles 7:14
Ezra 8:21–23
Psalms 17:8–9; 34:1–4; 35:4; 40:2–3; 65:1–5; 66:5; 81:1–7; 97:1–2; 103:1–18; 104:1–4; 124:1–8
Matthew 18:19–20
Acts 12:5
Philippians 4:6

98   What Price a Face?

A decision to grant less than £8,000 compensation to a little girl who was scarred for life received widespread criticism.

Francesca Quintyre was slashed in the face by a deranged man wielding a machete. The man attacked Francesca at her nursery school in Wolverhampton in 1996, and she was only rescued from worse injuries or death by her teacher Lisa Potts, who was later awarded the George Cross for her heroism.

Lisa, who nearly had her arm severed as she shielded the youngsters, branded the pay-out to Francesca, by the Criminal Injuries Compensation Board, 'disgusting'.

'Every day when she gets up and looks in the mirror she will see that terrible scar. It will be a constant reminder of the awful ordeal she was put through.'

Lisa added: 'It is an insult to offer her this amount of money. People who make these awards have no understanding of what it means to be the victim of savagery like this.'

The case has been taken up by solicitors who specialise in personal injury law suits. A spokesman for the legal team commented that if the injuries had been suffered in a car crash, Francesca would have received up to £40,000.

APPLICATION

What amount would you have given Francesca?

Ask everyone to repeat these phrases out loud after you: 'I am valuable, I am unique, I am special, I am amazing, I am mysterious, I am loved by God'.

How do we know that God loves us and values us? Is his love conditional on how we look, our abilities, our skills, or how we feel about ourselves?

THEMES

Appearance
Self-esteem
Suffering

BIBLE REFERENCES

Genesis 1:27
Psalm 139:13–14
Luke 15:1–7
1 Corinthians 3:16
Ephesians 2:6–10; 3:14–19
1 Peter 1:18–19

99   What's in a Name?

John Evans from Croydon had his £100,000 luxury holiday home in Costa del Sol sold without his knowledge by order of a Spanish court, because another man with the same name had failed to repay a loan for a television and could not be found. The innocent Mr Evans was furious to discover that the Spanish court refused to buy back his home.

In Canada, a similar case of mistaken identity has blighted a man for fifteen years. Charles Joseph Frederick, who lives near Calgary, had his home seized, his credit card rating shattered and was forced to pay child support payments after the Canadian government mistook him for another man of the same name.

'It doesn't help that my birth date is only two days different from his,' said the victim of the confusion. 'We were also both divorced in 1993 . . . they've been looking for him, but always find me.'

Mr Frederick described the experience as a 'nightmare', with agencies and bill collectors constantly harassing him for the shortcomings of his namesake. One government official suggested he change his name to avoid further trouble!

Meanwhile, researchers in the USA have discovered some incredibly unusual names: Ima Long comes from Texas, Katz Meow from Washington and a lady called Constant Agony lives in New York!

APPLICATION

Have you ever faced difficulties because of your name: for example, been teased or mistaken for someone else with the same name? Do you know what your Christian name means? How important is your name to you?

In some cultures a child is named according to a physical or personality characteristic; in others you inherit a parent's name. Mary and Joseph were told what name to give to the Christ-child: Jesus, meaning Saviour, because he would save the people from their sins. Isaiah also lists Christ's names: Wonderful, Counsellor, Mighty God, Everlasting Father, Prince of Peace (Isaiah 9:6).

God has given Jesus the name above all other names (Philippians 2:9–10).

Examples of biblical names and their meanings:

- Asher (happy) – Genesis 30:13

- Benjamin (son of my right hand) – Genesis 35:18

- Eliezer (God is my help) – Exodus 18:4

- Eve (life) – Genesis 3:20

- Ishmael (God hears) – Genesis 16:15

- Issachar (reward) – Genesis 30:18

- Judah (praise) – Genesis 29:35

- Mara (bitter) – Ruth 1:20

- Samuel (asked of God) – 1 Samuel 1:20

- Simeon (hearing) – Genesis 29:33

THEMES

Character of God
Choice
Identity
Names

BIBLE REFERENCES

Genesis 2:19–20; 32:29
Judges 13:17
Jeremiah 23:6
Matthew 1:21, 25; 2:23
Luke 1:31; 2:21
Acts 4:12
Revelation 19:12

100   Why I Staked My All

In 1991 Chris Boyd made the decision to gamble a huge amount of money on the spin of a roulette wheel. During the next three years he saved hard and sold his £124,000 house near Maidenhead, Berkshire. Then in 1994, with his friend Tony Litt, he set off for Las Vegas to gamble his life savings of £150,000 on one all-or-nothing bet! What's more, he didn't tell his girlfriend, June Hillhouse, where he was going and what he was going to do!

Tony and Chris went to Binion's Horseshoe, the only casino that would risk such a huge bet. He put all his chips on red – a 50/50 gamble.

He later told newspaper reporters: 'The ball went round. I felt nothing. It landed on red. Tony screamed "Yes!" I just sat there. People say I was Mr Cool – I was just Mr Numb.'

He went on to explain that it wasn't simply about risking a lot of money to make lots more. 'Some people climb Everest, others race motor bikes; this wasn't as crazy as any of those things,' he claimed. Source: *Today*

APPLICATION

What do you think about Chris Boyd's gamble – was he mad or courageous? How do you think his girlfriend felt when she found out? Is Chris right? Is climbing Everest or racing motorbikes crazier or riskier than gambling all your life savings on one 50/50 bet? What's the biggest risk that you have ever taken? How did you feel – nervous, cool, numb, scared?

Jesus claims that the biggest and craziest gamble a person

can take is ignoring God. He once told a story (Luke 12:13–21) of a man who worked hard and got rich. He then decided to take life easy, but having grown bumper crops, built large barns to store the food and prepared for early retirement, he suddenly died. Jesus described him as a fool for failing to pay attention to his spiritual welfare. You might think you play things safe, but if you leave God out of your life you are taking the biggest gamble you could ever take. Your eternal destiny hangs in the balance and you lose everything if you die without knowing God!

THEMES

Excitement
Gambling
Gospel
Money
Risk-taking

BIBLE REFERENCES

Numbers 27:21
1 Samuel 6:7–9
2 Chronicles 18:33–34
Proverbs 26:10
Ecclesiastes 2:17–19; 9:11
Luke 12:13–21

Index of Themes

Index of Bile References

50 Sketches about Jesus

by David Burt

Picture the scene: Jesus preaching at Wembley Stadium; a paparazzi photographer in Bethlehem; Mary cooking spaghetti hoops on toast; the wise men shopping in Harrods.

Strange? Maybe. Funny? Certainly. But every sketch highlights a truth about Jesus of Nazareth that is relevant to life today.

There's something here for all levels of expertise, and all ages. Fully indexed by themes, occasions and Bible references, this is an ideal resource for churches and other groups who wish to communicate old truths in fresh ways.